Peter Roe

C000093810

Tolkien the Pagan?
Reading Middle-earth
through a Spiritual Lens

Proceedings of The Tolkien Society
Seminar 2018

Edited by Anna Milon

Copyright © 2019 by The Tolkien Society
www.tolkiensociety.org

First published 2019 by Luna Press Publishing, Edinburgh
www.lunapresspublishing.com

ISBN-13: 978-1-911143-79-6

Cover illustration copyright © 2019 '*Starkindler*' by Becky Green
Published under the auspices of the Peter Roe Memorial Fund, eighteenth in the series.

All contributors to this volume assert their moral right to be identified as the author of
their individual contributions.

Each contribution remains the intellectual property of its respective author and is
published by The Tolkien Society, an educational charity (number 273809) registered
in England and Wales, under a non-exclusive licence.

All rights reserved by The Tolkien Society. No part of this publication may be
reproduced, stored in a retrieval system, or transmitted in any form or by any means,
electronic, mechanical, photocopy, recording or otherwise, without prior written
permission of the copyright holder. Nor can it be circulated in any form of binding or
cover other than that in which it is published and without similar condition including
this condition being imposed on a subsequent purchaser.

Contents

About the Peter Roe Memorial Fund

The Tolkien Society's seminar proceedings and other booklets are typically published under the auspices of the Peter Roe Memorial Fund, a fund in the Society's accounts that commemorates a young member who died in a traffic accident. Peter Roe, a young and very talented person joined the Society in 1979, shortly after his sixteenth birthday. He had discovered Middle-earth some time earlier, and was so inspired by it that he even developed his own system of runes, similar to the Dwarvish Angerthas, but which utilised logical sound values, matching the logical shapes of the runes. Peter was also an accomplished cartographer, and his bedroom was covered with multi-coloured maps of the journeys of the fellowship, plans of Middle-earth, and other drawings.

Peter was also a creative writer in both poetry and prose—the subject being incorporated into his own *Dwarvish Chronicles*. He was so enthusiastic about having joined the Society that he had written a letter ordering all the available back issues, and was on his way to buy envelopes when he was hit by a speeding lorry outside his home.

Sometime later, Jonathan and Lester Simons (at that time Chairman and Membership Secretary respectively) visited Peter's parents to see his room and to look at the work on which he had spent so much care and attention in such a tragically short life. It was obvious that Peter had produced, and would have continued to produce, material of such a high standard as to make a complete booklet, with poetry, calligraphy, stories and cartography. The then committee set up a special account in honour of Peter, with the consent of his parents, which would be the source of finance for the Society's special publications. Over the years a number of members have made generous donations to the fund.

The first publication to be financed by the Peter Roe Memorial Fund was *Some Light on Middle-earth* by Edward Crawford, published in 1985. Subsequent publications have been composed from papers delivered at Tolkien Society workshops and seminars, talks from guest speakers at the Annual Dinner, and collections of the best articles from past issues of *Amon Hen*, the Society's bulletin.

Dwarvish Fragments, an unfinished tale by Peter, was printed in *Mallorn* 15 (September 1980). A standalone collection of Peter's creative endeavours is currently being prepared for publication.

The Peter Roe Series

Conventions and Abbreviations

Citations to Tolkien's works are provided inline and use the following abbreviations. Because there are so many editions of *The Hobbit* and *The Lord of the Rings*, citations are by volume, book, and chapter only. Similarly, references to the appendices of *The Lord of the Rings* are by appendix, section, and subsection only. All other references are provided in footnotes according to the *MHRA Style Guide*. Bibliographies of all works consulted (other than Tolkien's works listed below) are found at the end of most chapters.

A&I	*The Lay of Aotrou and Itroun*, ed. by Verlyn Flieger (London: HarperCollins, 2016)
Arthur	*The Fall of Arthur,* ed. by Christopher Tolkien (London: HarperCollins, 2013; Boston: Houghton Mifflin Harcourt, 2013)
AW	*Ancrene Wisse* (Oxford: Oxford University Press, 1962)
B&L	*Beren and Lúthien*, ed. by Christopher Tolkien (London: HarperCollins, 2017)
Beowulf	*Beowulf: A Translation and Commentary, together with Sellic Spell*, ed. by Christopher Tolkien (London: HarperCollins, 2014; Boston: Houghton Mifflin Harcourt, 2014)
Bombadil	*The Adventures of Tom Bombadil and other verses from the Red Book* (London: George Allen &

Unwin, 1962; Boston: Houghton Mifflin, 1962)

CoH   *The Children of Húrin*, ed. by Christopher Tolkien
               (London: HarperCollins, 2007; Boston: Houghton
               Mifflin Harcourt, 2007)

Exodus   *The Old English Exodus*, ed. by Joan Turville-Petre
               (Oxford: Oxford University Press, 1982)

Father Christmas Letters from Father Christmas, ed. by Baillie
               Tolkien (London: George Allen & Unwin, 1976;
               Boston: Houghton Mifflin, 1976)

FoG   *The Fall of Gondolin*, ed. by Christopher Tolkien
               (London: HarperCollins, 2018).

FR   *The Fellowship of the Ring*

Hobbit   *The Hobbit*

Jewels   *The War of the Jewels,* ed. by Christopher Tolkien
               (London: HarperCollins, 1994; Boston: Houghton
               Mifflin, 1994)

Kullervo   *The Story of Kullervo,* ed. by Verlyn Flieger
               (London: HarperCollins, 2015; Boston: Houghton
               Mifflin Harcourt, 2016)

Lays   *The Lays of Beleriand,* ed. by Christopher Tolkien
               (London: George Allen & Unwin, 1985; Boston:
               Houghton Mifflin, 1985)

Letters   *The Letters of J.R.R. Tolkien,* ed. by Humphrey
               Carpenter with the assistance of Christopher

Perilous Realm   *Tales from the Perilous Realm* (London: HarperCollins, 1997)

RK   *The Return of the King*

Silmarillion   *The Silmarillion*, ed. by Christopher Tolkien (London: George Allen & Unwin, 1977; Boston: Houghton Mifflin, 1977).

Sauron   *Sauron Defeated*, ed. by Christopher Tolkien (London: HarperCollins, 1992; Boston: Houghton Mifflin, 1992)

Secret Vice   *A Secret Vice: Tolkien on Invented Languages*, ed. by Dimitra Fimi and Andrew Higgins (London: HarperCollins, 2016)

Shadow   *The Return of the Shadow*, ed. by Christopher Tolkien (London: Unwin Hyman, 1988; Boston: Houghton Mifflin, 1988)

Shaping   *The Shaping of Middle-earth*, ed. by Christopher Tolkien (London: George Allen & Unwin, 1986; Boston: Houghton Mifflin, 1986)

S&G   *The Legend of Sigurd and Gudrún*, ed. by Christopher Tolkien (London: HarperCollins, 2009; Boston: Houghton Mifflin Harcourt, 2009)

TL   *Tree and Leaf*, 2nd edn (London: Unwin Hyman, 1988; Boston: Houghton Mifflin, 1989)

TT   *The Two Towers*

Treason	*The Treason of Isengard*, ed. by Christopher Tolkien (London: Unwin Hyman; Boston: Houghton Mifflin, 1989)
UT	*Unfinished Tales of Númenor and Middle-earth*, ed. by Christopher Tolkien (London: George Allen & Unwin, 1980; Boston: Houghton Mifflin, 1980)
War	*The War of the Ring*, ed. by Christopher Tolkien (London: Unwin Hyman, 1990; Boston: Houghton Mifflin, 1990)

Introduction

Anna Milon

The topic for the Tolkien Society 2018 seminar – 'Tolkien the Pagan? Reading Middle-earth through a Spiritual Lens' – arose from a place of curiosity regarding the place of spirituality in fantasy. Tolkien is in the minority among fantasy authors as one who has no defined religion or cult implicit within his fictional universe. And yet the richness of the world of Arda lends itself to being read through multiple spiritual lenses. Arda allows both for the second coming of Eru, as discussed by Finrod and Andreth in *Athrabeth Finrod ah Andreth*, and the totem-like Púkel-men; contains both the monotheistic cosmogony of Eru proclaiming 'Ea!' – the world that is, and the pantheistic ideas of the voice of Nimrodel, an elven maiden lost to the world, dwelling eternally in the stream that bears her name. Such a world reflects Tolkien's own complex relationship with magic and 'the old songs of other pagan days [that] have stirred other Christians' to new poetry (*Kullervo*).

However, all such discussions inevitably snag on the much-quoted lines from one of Tolkien's letters: 'The Lord of the Rings is of course a fundamentally religious and Catholic work; unconsciously so at first, but consciously in the revision' (*Letters*, Letter 142). In the particular case of this Seminar's topic, these words were taken by certain individuals to mean that Tolkien was a Catholic who wrote works for Catholics about Catholic matters and to see his fiction in any other light is somewhat embarrassing. While the first point stands without dispute, the rest of the argument is negated by Tolkien's own admission that 'I am in any case myself a Christian; but the "third age" [of Arda] was not a Christian world' (Ibid., Letter 165).

Ronald Hutton elegantly deescalates the conflict between those arguing the Christian reading of Tolkien's fiction being the only one with any veracity and those espousing a more critically diverse approach by stating that 'Tolkien himself did not in fact pay such attention when he wrote his fiction, tending instead to write instinctively and to draw in the process on other traditions, more favourable to magic than the established Christian one' (Hutton, 144).

Unfortunately, the notion of Tolkien stirred to new poetry by pre-Christian sources also fails to satisfy, as C. R. Carmichael writes on his blog that Tolkien was tragically blind to 'the fatal spiritual consequences of his creative endeavours'. The result of these endeavours for Carmichael is that 'Neo-Pagans, Gnostics and other occult-based religionists absolutely adore Tolkien's works, but are not turning to Christianity for spiritual understanding', as he is effectively complaining that *The Lord of the Rings* is bad conversion literature (*The Sad Truth of Tolkien Spirituality*). However, in trying to gatekeep against non-Christian and non-theistic interpretations, individuals like Carmichael drew attention to the complex relationship between the readers of Middle-earth and spirituality, which was skilfully explored by the delegates at the Tolkien Society Seminar 2018.

The Seminar, which took place on the 1st of July at the Hilton Leeds City Hotel, was the largest to date, both by number of delegates and number of papers. The thirteen papers presented ranged from studies of Christian Providence manifesting in the ages of Arda to the correspondences between members of the Fellowship and Chakras. The keynote speaker, Markus Altena Davidsen, addressed the question of Tolkien's writing as a foundation for a religious movement in 'Honouring the Valar, Seeking the Elf Within…' and his paper is reproduced in this volume alongside Aslı Bülbül Candaş's pantheistic exploration of Arda's natural world, Ryan Haecker's paper on Providence and Historicism in Middle-earth, Giovanni Carmine Costabile's unconventional reading of Tolkien's work through the lens of Nietzschean philosophy and Justin Lewis-Anthony discussion of death as a being and as natural phenomenon in the writing of Tolkien and Pratchett.

On behalf of The Tolkien Society, I would like to extend my gratitude to the delegates and presenters of the Tolkien Society Seminar 2018, without whom this event would not have been possible, and to the Tolkien Society committee for facilitating the organisation of the Seminar. This publication is made possible by the generosity of the Peter Roe memorial fund.

Bibliography

Carmichael, C. R. 'The Sad Truth of Tolkien's Spirituality.' *Sacred Sandwich*, 26 October 2017. http://sacredsandwich.com/2017/10/26/the-sad-truth-of-tolkien-spirituality/ [accessed 5 December 2018]

Hutton, Ronald. 'Tolkien's Magic' *Year's Work in Medievalism*. 2016, pp. 144 – 153.

Tolkien, J. R. R. *The Letters of J.R.R. Tolkien*. Edited by Humphrey Carpenter with the assistance of Christopher Tolkien, Houghton Mifflin, 2000.

---. *The Story of Kullervo*. Edited by Verlyn Flieger, HarperCollins, 2015.

On the Providential Historicism of Middle-earth

Ryan Haecker

The Providence and Historicism of Middle-earth

The theme of history, in J.R.R. Tolkien's mythopoeia, echoes beneath the panoply of sights and sounds, like a baritone that bellows its horn in the recollections of stories and songs. Remembrances of antique things then pierce through the panoply of the present, peek into the narrative, and enchant the imagination of the reader. And as the story of *The Lord of the Rings* develops from the initial intrigues of Hobbiton to a global strategic conflict, the reader finds that the limited ordeals of the Fellowship are merely a microcosm that reflects a universal historical drama for the future of Middle-earth. Yet as this historical drama draws to its conclusion, its part within the symbolic concert rises to a new crescendo, so that the theme of historicism can be heard to contribute to the movement of providential restoration.

The characters, like the readers, of *The Lord of the Rings* may, thereafter, reflect upon this history of Middle-earth from a late historical perspective, like that which we the children of modernity may now look upon our past. The procession of the ages is then one that has passed, and also one that may now only be recollected as it can be re-narrated. Each age then expresses a new theme: for if the First Age recalls an antediluvian or Homeric era of springtime Elves and heroic first Men; and the Second Age bespeaks a classical era of expansive empires, then the Third Age more resembles a dissolute era of pygmies rather than of heroes and of social decline rather than of imperial grandeur.

Each ensuing age then repeats this conflicted cycle from the fall to the restoration: in the First Age, Fëanor and the Noldor Elves departed Valinor to make war on Melkor, to possess the wide lands of Middle-earth, and to reclaim the Silmarils; in the Second Age, the Men of Númenor were empowered beyond their capacity for judicious restraint and, after many centuries of industrial and imperial expansion, sought to acquire measureless riches and overcome the limits of human mortality; and in the Third Age, the nations of Gondor and Arnor were slowly enervated and debilitated through illusory pride, possessiveness and indolence, before, at the end, the One Ring was destroyed; the Dark Lord was toppled; and the free peoples of Middle-earth were reunited for the restoration of the world.

These repeated cycles from the fall to the restoration can be read to trace the providence and historicism of Middle-earth. *Historicism* is a mode of interpreting history according to an intuition of the plurality of forces developing within and amongst the historical life-cycle of nations. Although this term is often associated with the radical relativity of all historical concepts, it may more fruitfully be understood, in both a more basic and a more general sense, as the theory of history for which universal and reoccurring historical patterns may determine any interpretation of events. Historicism can thus be conceived as the eternal logic of the causes of historical change that shapes the sequence of all events in history.

Providence is the theory that the divine intellect directs the sequence of events in human history. The history of Middle-earth is narrated by Tolkien as it proceeds from these eternal ideas of the divine intellect for such a providential purpose (Dubs 1981, 135). The providence of the history of Middle-earth is, as I will describe, orchestrated by the three themes of the Great Music of the Ainur to shape a series of cyclical patterns, within which long-term social and political decline may at last be providentially remedied by an episodic succession of partial restorations.

Tolkien's providential historicism seems however to have been strangely neglected. Many scholars have observed these themes, but most have so far neglected to elaborate upon their theological dimension. Gunnar Urang, in "Tolkien's Fantasy: The Phenomenology of Hope" (1969), first pointed to the providential historicism of Middle-earth. Randel Helms, in *Tolkien's World* (1974), also lists five internal laws of Middle-earth, of which the first is that of providence. Kathleen E. Dubs, in "Providence, Fate, and Chance: Boethian Philosophy in The Lord of the Rings" (1981), has perhaps, most influentially, examined the Boethian themes of 'providence, fate, chance, and free will' in Tolkien's mythopoeia.

Stephen Smith, in "Providence And Free Will In The History Of J.R.R. Tolkien's Middle-Earth" (1980), has similarly argued that Tolkien's historicism is "patterned after Christian concepts of history"; universalized in a divine origin; and periodicized into the first, second, and third ages that may be demarcated by the epoch-making events of eucatastrophe in expectation of a 'limited' eschatological end. The horizon of historicism thus appears as that of the eschaton; of the Second Great Music;

7

and of its final fulfilment in the Music and Mind of Ilúvatar. Tolkien's historicism has thus been called providential, and his providence Christian, even as its theological themes have yet to be explored. I wish, with what follows, to trace this theme to the Great Music of the Ainur, the liminal traces of Tolkien's trinitarian theology, and the theological dimension of the providential historicism of Middle-earth.

The Proto-Trinitarian Evangelium of the Ainulindale

The key theological text of Tolkien's trinitarian theology can, I suggest, be found in the first chapter of the Silmarillion, the account of the creation of the cosmos, and the music of the Ainur, or the Ainulindalë. This Great Music of the Ainur appears to exhibit the traces of Tolkien's trinitarian theology. For he here presents a narrative of the birth of the cosmos, a cosmogony, involving the three distinct divine personae: Ilúvatar the 'father of all'; the Great Music flowing forth from the divine Mind; and the Flame Imperishable that is sent to kindle the fiery freedom of his children in creation.

These three divine personae can be correlated with those of Christian trinitarian theology: God the Father appears as Ilúvatar; Christ the Son as the divine Mind; and the Holy Spirit as the Flame Imperishable. Tolkien's mythopoeia can then be re-read to distinguish these three divine personae, like the Old Testament *protoevangelium* that foreshadowed the coming of Christ, without, however, explicitly naming them prior to any anticipated historical revelation.

Tolkien initially signals a proleptic foreshadowing of divine plurality in unity. He writes, in the first line, "There was Eru, the One, who in Arda is called Ilúvatar; and he made first the Ainur,

8

the Holy Ones, that were the offspring of his thought, and they were with him before aught else was made" (*Silmarillion*, 3). Eru, the One, is one, and yet, also, the one who, by begetting the Ainur and creating Arda can be called Ilúvatar, the 'father of all'.

Ilúvatar is, here, the first begetter, while the Ainur are the first begotten children of Ilúvatar. The Ainur are, however, plurally begotten, not from Ilúvatar alone, but, as 'offspring of his thought', and from the 'mind of Ilúvatar', which, by begetting, is already itself other than Ilúvatar. The 'Mind of Ilúvatar', by begetting the Ainur as many from one, is, at precisely this point, already other as it is embedded in a plural relation of one to many, where the Mind is itself other than the One, and, as such, is many in one. This divine intellect can thus be distinguished, like Christ the Son of the Johannine *Logos*, by the first difference that is also at once the first relation from God the 'father of all' Ilúvatar.

The Ainulindalë begins before the creation of the world as though it were an angelic rehearsal of history. The first theme is created through the cooperation of the faithful Ainur. The second theme is created by the conflict between the followers of the rebellious Melkor and the obedient Manwë. The dissonance of this counter-theme then introduces disharmony and cacophony into the Great Music (*Morgoth's Ring*, 406). And the attempted usurpation of divine sovereignty thereafter enacts the first and prototypical rebellion with which evil may be irreparably introduced into the created cosmos. The third theme – introduced through the power of Ilúvatar alone – then reconciles the first and second theme into a 'solemn pattern, blended of sorrow and beauty' (*Silmarillion*, 17). These three themes can then correspond to cosmic concord, discord, and

9

harmony, where, through the alterior malevolence of discord, both may be mixed for a more rich and glorious melody.

Ilúvatar creates the Ainur so as to freely cooperate in this orchestration. He raises his left hand – the hand on the side of the other – and smiles to signal the conclusion of the oppositive otherness of the first theme, and he raises his right hand – the hand on the side of the self – and weeps to signal the conflictual coincidence of the second and third theme, with which both opposites can be cancelled and combined in and by the final theme. Yet, at the height of discord, Ilúvatar rings one 'unfathomed chord' to reconcile this absolute opposition. The cacophonous discord that momentarily disrupts the polyphony of the first and second theme is thus eternally harmonized in and by this third theme. The Great Music can thereafter constitute an angelic chorus, with which the Ainur can compose, for the as yet uncreated cosmos of Eä, the eternal archetype of the temporal unfolding of the successive stages in the providential historicism of Middle-earth.

Ilúvatar then shows the Ainur a vision of the as yet uncreated history of Middle-earth. The Ainur can, by this vision, see the effects of their own contributions to the three themes of the Great Music, even as none of the Ainur can then see what is to be willed by the freedom of Ilúvatar, nor of the Ainur, nor indeed of any of his children. The degree of their prescient foreknowledge is, in this way, limited to their own creative contributions to the Ainulindalë, which can, consequently, never afterwards extend to any foreknowledge of the free subcreation of the other children of Ilúvatar.

Freedom enters into creation with this Great Music. For the children of Ilúvatar are said to have been created, not by the Ainur, but by this very paradoxical coincidence of providence and of freedom with the third theme of the Ainulindalë. The children of Ilúvatar are, accordingly, not the products of the Ainur, nor of any Gnostic sub-creation – not even the dwarves who are animated as from above – but rather and only of this primary divine creation, which is an expression of the freedom of divinity; of divine difference; and of the gift, through the first divine difference of the Mind of Ilúvatar, and of the second divine difference of the Secret Fire that kindles the freedom of the world with all of its creatures.

Human freedom may, then, be treated as a more radical expressions of this gift of divine freedom. For the 'strange gift' of Men is, Tolkien indicates, such a gift to 'go beyond' the 'original Music of the Ainur' and freely choose to oppose the apparent pattern of the divine design and providential historicism of the three themes of the Great Music. It is through this gift of freedom, that Men may thereafter begin to exceed so as to enact new and never yet foreseen changes to the history of Middle-earth. And since it is these three themes of the Great Music that may also providentially direct any alterity and contingency in history from and for the sovereign purpose of Ilúvatar, all of the changes made by Men can ultimately and cumulatively contribute to the final fruition of the providential historicism of Middle-earth.

Following the Great Music, Ilúvatar proclaims to the Ainur: 'I will send forth into the Void the Flame imperishable and it shall be at the heart of the World' (*Silmarillion*, 20). The Great Music is, at this conclusion of the Ainulindalë, thus imbued with the Flame Imperishable to become the living historical cosmos of Eä. And Ilúvatar afterwards indicates the providential plan of the history of Arda when he remarks: 'even Melkor will discover those things there which he thought to contrive of his

11

own heart, out of harmony with my mind, and he will find them but a part of the whole and tributary to its glory.' For the three themes of the Ainulindalë can then be recapitulated as these themes unfold through its story, of its tragedies, and of the succession of stages with which we can trace the providential historicism of Middle-earth.

The Historicism of Middle-earth

The three themes of the Ainulindalë can create an eternal pattern of the successive stages that cyclically cascade through the whole history of Middle-earth. The three themes then produce three Aeons demarcated by three light sources, just as it produces three ages that are demarcated by three cataclysms. And this triadic pattern of history may thereafter non-identically repeat the triple relations of the three themes of the Great Music in a vestigial image of the three divine personae of what we can call Tolkien's trinitarian theology.

Recollections of the purpose of providence are, admittedly, incompletely and imperfectly narrated: for it appears, at first, to be limited by the imperfect foreknowledge of the angelic Ainur. Tolkien hints that their foreknowledge extends no further than the end of the Third Age when he writes: 'some have said that the vision ceased ere the fulfilment of the Dominion of Men and the fading of the Firstborn; wherefore, though the Music is over all, the Valar have not seen as with sight of the Later Ages or the ending of the World' (*Silmarillion*, 5). This passage, at the start of the Silmarillion, suggests that, since foreknowledge of the historicism of Middle-earth is limited to the Third Age, the climax of this narrative drama at the conclusion of *The Lord of the Rings* marks the horizon of the furthest future.

The historicism of Middle-earth may thus be bounded at its furthest future by the horizon of the Third Age, with nothing beyond it but a looming expectation of the eschaton. We can thus distinguish three Aeons demarcated by three distinct light sources from the three Ages that epochally periodize the history of Middle-earth: the three Aeons of the elder days are followed, in the third Aeon of the Sun and Moon, by the three Ages, which can culminate in the conclusion of the Third Age, the destruction of the One Ring, and the reunion of the Kingdom of Men. The three Aeons and the three Ages, can then, for Tolkien as for Augustine, then plausibly correspond to the six days of creation, at the end of *The Lord of the Rings*, in anticipation of the eschatological end, concluding with the final battle of *Dagor Dagorath*, and of the breaking of the world, when, Tolkien hints, all of the free creatures will come to contribute a Second Great Music with which the world may at last be restored.

The history of Arda can, accordingly, be periodized by the succession of three light-sources that illuminate the world. Verilyn Flieger has influentially described how the languages and societies of Elves and Men signify something of this luminous emanation from Ilúvatar to Arda (Flieger, 1983, 69). The ensuing geographic divisions of Elves and Men then fragment and disrupt the harmony of languages and societies: the first light-source is that of the Two Lamps held aloft by the highest peaks of Illuin and Ormal; the second is the Two Trees that illuminate only Valinor; and the third is the Sun and the Moon that circle and illuminate the globe of Arda. (Flieger, 1983, 75) The first, second, and third ages, thereafter, transpire within this third aeon of the Sun and the Moon. These three Aeons and Ages of the history of Middle-earth can thus be read to cycle through the following three historicist cycles of the societies of Elves and Men.

The history of the First Age depicts the destruction of the Two Trees and the theft of the Silmarils by Melkor, the consequent rebellion of Fëanor, and the ensuing exodus of the elven race of the Noldor from the land of Valinor. The Silmarils are the three irreplaceable crystals that uniquely capture and radiate the brilliant light of the Two Trees (Flieger, 1983, 94, 100). Through the rebellion of Fëanor, the First Age exhibits the alienation of Elven society from Ilúvatar in Middle-Earth. But by the inspired heroism and consummate union of the three men and elf-maidens the First Age also produces a reconciliation of Elves, Men and the Valar. For within the historicist cycle of the First Age, the rebellion of Fëanor has the significance of a fall from original grace, while the heroism of the three unions of elves and men has the further significance of a providential reconciliation of the peoples of Middle-earth with Ilúvatar.

The history of the Second Age then depicts the prodigious development of this first great kingdom of Men, the Isle of Númenor, their rebellion against the Valar, and the defeat of Sauron during the War of the Last Alliance. The far-sighted men of the isle of Númenor - midway between blessed Valinor and Middle-earth - most resembled the splendour of the first Elves; who were themselves most like the Valar of all the creatures of Arda. They prodigiously ascended to dizzying heights of sophistication, prosperity and refinement. Yet their talent and achievement only intensified their growing discontent with the uninvited horizons of mortality. When their never-since equalled majesty thereafter disposed them to become ever more unwilling to relinquish the fruits of life for the uncertain perils of death, they abandoned reverence for Ilúvatar to naked blasphemy, attempted to invade the immortal lands of Valinor, and were doomed by the cataclysmic drowning of the isle of Númenor.

The history of Gondor in the Third Age from Elendil to Denethor presents a lengthy historical decline from the resplendent days of the kings to the uncertain times of the stewards. The lonely defence of the south-easterly battlements of Minas Tirith recalls the one thousand-year defence and preservation of antique culture within the great fortress-city of Constantinople. The organic continuity of the Kingdom of Gondor is here symbolized by the White Tree of Gondor. The White Tree is rooted before the hall of the kings in the uppermost courtyard of Minas Tirith where it is guarded as a totemic representation of the nation's vitality. It is, like the King himself, elevated and revered above all others due to its extraordinary divine nature. The diminution of Gondor's national vitality is thus embodied in the death of the White Tree, the absence of the kings, and the enervation and aimlessness of the ruling steward Denethor; whose suicidal descent into the richly ornamented tombs of Gondor's Kings recalls the catastrophic sinking of Númenor.

The history of Middle-earth thus illustrates a succession of historicist cycles wherein rebellion and decline are providentially remedied through the climactic episodes of heroic restorations. Each of these historicist cycles contain three moments which are providentially directed by the three themes of the Great Music: for in the first moment, societies are produced which faithfully resemble the original harmony of Ilúvatar; in the second moment, a faction within society rebels and, by their wilful activity towards independence from the whole, fragments and introduces discordant evil within that society; yet in the third act, inspired heroes collect from amongst these fragments a small part of the essence and substance of the first moment, and, by its totemic power, achieve a miraculous victory over all opponents. These three moments can thereafter come to produce a new society, which, while containing what is essential to the first moment, has, moreover, been transformed in and through this struggle with the second moment, in such a way as to be ennobled and enriched by the whole history and heroism of the past.

This triadic pattern of the providential historicism of Middle-earth evidently mirrors the triplicity of Tolkien's trinitarian theology. The three Ages are circumscribed in time by the three Aeons, just as these three Aeons and three Ages are altogether orchestrated by the Great Music and animated by the Flame Imperishable. The triadic pattern of history can then be collected into the three moments, themes, and divine personae. The three Aeons, Ages, and, most of all, the narrative climax of this conflict between providence and freedom, then reflexively imitate the three themes of the Ainulindalë, where the discord of tragedy is turned to the harmony of a eucatastrophe, and the divine difference of the Mind of Ilúvatar is made into the music of history in time. Each epochal eucatastrophe may then come to reconcile the malevolent alterity of freedom in and for the beneficence of divine providence. The providential historicism of Middle-earth is, in its reconciliation with freedom, not at all foreknown as determined, but, rather, the spiritual reconciliation of this supplemental surplus, which, while exceeding the surplus vision of the Ainur, flows forth from the triplicity of moments as it is orchestrated in the Ainulindalë by the three divine personae.

Bibliography

Tolkien the Medievalist. Edited by Jane Chance, Routledge, 2003.

Birzer, Bradley J. *J. R. R. Tolkien's Sanctifying Myth: Understanding Middle-Earth*. ISI, 2002.

Chance, Jane. *Tolkien and the Invention of Myth: A Reader*. University of Kentucky, 2004.

Cox, John. "Tolkien's Platonic Fantasy." *Seven: An Anglo-American Literary Review*. 1984, pp. 53 – 69.

Dubs, Kathleen E. "Providence, Fate, and Chance: Boethian Philosophy in *The Lord of the Rings*." *Twentieth Century Literature*, vol. 27, no. 1, 1981, pp. 34 – 42.

Flieger, Verlyn. *Splintered Light: Logos and Language in Tolkien's World*. Eerdmans, 1983.

--- "Naming the Unnameable: The Neoplatonic 'One' in Tolkien's *Silmarillion*." *Diakonia: Studies in Honor of Robert T. Meyer*. Edited by Thomas Halton and Joseph P. Williman, Catholic University of America Press, 1986, pp. 127-132.

Freeh, Helen Lasseter. "On Fate, Providence, And Free Will in *The Silmarillion*." *Tolkien Among The Moderns*. Edited by Ralph C. Wood, University Of Notre Dame Press, 2015.

Garbowski, Christopher. "The History of Middle-Earth." *Mallorn: The Journal of the Tolkien Society*, vol. 37, no. 37, 1999, pp. 20 – 25.

Halsall, Michael. *A Critical Assessment Of The Influence Of Neoplatonism In J.R.R. Tolkien's Philosophy Of Life As 'Being And Gift'*, Doctoral Dissertation, University of Nottingham, 2016.

Ivey, Christin. "The Presence of Divine Providence in the Absence of "God":

The Role of Providence, Fate, and Free Will in Tolkien Mythology", *The Corinthian: The Journal of Student Research* at GCSU, 9, 2, 2008.

Koons, Robert. "Tolkien's Wizardry: How Metaphysics Molded Middle-Earth, 2006." (Unpublished)

Madsen, Catherine. "Light from an Invisible Lamp: Natural Religion in The Lord of the Rings". *Mythlore*, vol. 14, 1988, pp. 43 – 47.

Mcintosh, Jonathan S. *The Flame Imperishable: Tolkien, St. Thomas, And The Metaphysics Of Faerie*, Dissertation, University of Dallas, 2009.

McPartland, Thomas J. "The Lord of the Rings: Mythopoesis, Heroism and Providence.", *The American Political Science Association Annual Conference*, Seattle, September, 2011.

Mitchell, C.I. "Legend and History Have Met and Fused: The Interlocution of Anthropology, Historiography, and Incarnation. JRR Tolkien's 'On Fairy-stories'". *Tolkien Studies*, West Virginia University Press, 2011.

Nagy, Gergely. "Saving the Myths: the Recreation of Mythology in Plato and Tolkien". *Tolkien and the Invention of Myth: A Reader*, 2004.

Nitzsche, Jane Chance. *Tolkien's Art: A Mythology for England*. London: Macmillan, 1980.

Scull, Christina. "The History of Middle-Earth." *Seven: An Anglo-American Literary Review*, vol. 12, no. 12, 1995, pp. 105 – 127.

Smith, Stephen P. *Providence And Free Will In The History Of J.R.R. Tolkien's Middle-Earth*, Masters Thesis: Western Kentucky University.

Tolkien, J. R. R. *The Letters of J.R.R. Tolkien*. Edited by Humphrey Carpenter with the assistance of Christopher Tolkien, Houghton Mifflin, 2000.

--- *The Lord of the Rings*. Houghton Mifflin, 2002.

--- *Morgoth's Ring: The Later Silmarillion, the Legends of Aman.* Houghton Mifflin, 1993.

--- *Tree and Leaf.* Harper Collins Publishers, 2001.

--- *The Silmarillion.* Houghton Mifflin, 1977.

The Nature of Arda: An Artwork as the Embodiment of the Flame Imperishable

Aslı Bülbül Candaş

In Tolkien's secondary world, every story gains meaning through the embodiment of Arda. The Music of the Ainur is played to exhibit a vision, and Ilúvatar reveals this vision to the Ainur in order for them to create Arda in the ontological realm. Their music celebrates the meaning of life in the middle of the Void, and as for *The Silmarillion*, this meaning is hidden in the power of creation. Known as the Flame Imperishable, the same flame of creative power that stays with the mind of Ilúvatar repeats itself in Arda's nature; thus along with its planetary existence, this secondary world becomes a presentation of the belief in the power of creation hidden in the natural world of Arda Tolkien's mythology becomes more complete as this facet of nature is practiced by Arda's denizens through art and craft to manifest nature's glory and uniqueness. Nature is definitely a separate entity in Arda, but it needs many agencies to reveal its inner, Secret Fire through arts, crafts and shaping natural formations from the outside. From this aspect, the creative deeds of Yavanna, Fëanor, Melian, Celebrimbor and Galadriel have the utmost importance. All the things they do reveal the Flame Imperishable in their own way. Apart from various subjective interpretations of the concept of religion in Tolkien's secondary world, many characters simply believe in the blessedness of

Arda as a concrete realm from its very beginning: "But when the Ainur had beheld this habitation in a vision and had seen the Children of Ilúvatar … then many of the most mighty … desire towards that place" (*Silmarillion*, 18). They accept Arda as their home, which houses and protects them and supports their creativity with its own boundless sources of creation, and in return they devote their lives to the immortalisation of the creative power in nature.

Before Tolkien's secondary world comes into being as a physical realm, there is the Music of the Ainur and the vision of a new World as a reflection of this music. These stages constitute and emphasise a process of creation which will end up with Arda having its own physical qualities, the most obvious of which is its nature. Therefore, both the Music and the vision become telic and highlight what will come after. In *Ainulindalë*, which is the cosmogony narrative of Tolkien's legendarium, there is a parade of different creative practices from the very beginning. Aside from the human author building a secondary world through words, first we "read" about "Music", which is followed by a "vision" and a physical existence in the end. Language, music and image come together to bring forward an idea of Arda along with its "roaring of the sea", "the winds and the air, and the matters of which Arda was made, of iron and stone and silver and gold and many substances" (ibid., 19). The nature of Arda is the ultimate artistic creation in the legendarium in the sense that it will be the sole setting and origin for all artworks that will come after.

In this process of creation, the status and journey of the Flame Imperishable have utmost importance as this concept accompanies the whole process. At first, the Flame Imperishable is with the Godhead Eru Ilúvatar as he kindles the Ainur with it. Once the Ainur are created from it, they also have power of creation but to a limited extent, as the Flame Imperishable still stays with Ilúvatar. That is how they make the Music but cannot put more creative power into practice beyond it without the guidance of Ilúvatar. Later on, Ilúvatar sends "forth into the Void the Flame Imperishable, and it shall be at the heart of the World, and the World shall Be" (ibid., 20). From this point on, every kind of creative power takes place within the boundaries of this World since the Flame Imperishable as the flame of creative power finds its ultimate residence at the core of Arda. The nature of Arda is the only visible and accessible facet of the Flame Imperishable for Arda's denizens, and it is more than a physical concept and existence. Besides carrying the Secret Fire deep within, it hosts many beings putting their own lesser creative power into practice, and various artworks as the outcome of this process reflect but a small portion of this Fire in varying degrees. That's how the nature of Arda becomes an artwork itself over time by being cultivated and forged in various ways to reveal its living, inner Flame Imperishable. It is given a spirit by Ilúvatar but it needs many other creatures to believe in its creative power to have its spiritual existence revealed.

This spiritual side is present even before Arda comes into physical existence. The completion of Arda is a long labour divided between the Valar; "it was their task to achieve it," (*Silmarillion*, 25) and each Vala has their sole commitment to a separate part in Arda's nature. This situation attributes to this planetary realm a spiritual existence beyond being just a physical setting. Arda ensouls its own inner life in the form of the Flame Imperishable, and reveals the physical aspects of this secret fire through waters, lands, earth, air and many other facets of nature on the surface. All these physical facets manifest their unique levels and ways of spirituality via the Vala by whom they have been shaped, ordered and controlled: "the voice of Manwë as a mighty wind" and "if the Children of Eru beheld him [Ulmo] they were filled with a great dread; for the arising of the King of the Sea was terrible, as a mounting wave" (ibid., 26, 37). Nevertheless, all the effort of the Valar is composed of exhibiting the creative power of nature by realizing their potential and more significantly, by fulfilling Arda's own potential in return, which is declared to them by the vision. This relationship is obvious in the way Yavanna is described: "Some there are who have seen her standing like a tree under heaven, crowned with the Sun … but the roots of the tree were in the waters of Ulmo, and the winds of Manwë spoke in its leaves" (ibid., 27 – 28). The Flame Imperishable wants to manifest itself through the nature of Arda, and it relies on the Valar to produce revelatory artworks by believing in the nature's creative power.

In the beginning of days, the Valar first represent different elements of the nature on their own. It is almost like a discovery of the creative potential of Arda's nature. Then they start to create things out of it and artistic creation begins in the literal sense. The first obvious artwork based on Arda's nature is the Two Trees created by Yavanna's song. The Flame in the heart of Arda surfaces in the light in the Two Trees: "…from each of his (Telperion) countless flowers a dew of silver light was ever falling … Flowers swung upon her (Laurelin) branches in clusters of yellow flame … and from the blossom of that tree there came forth warmth and a great light" (ibid., 38). With this first manifestation of the inner Flame of Arda, that is, with the first revelation of its spirit, begins the Count of Time, then the creation story of the Silmarils, followed by the exile of the Noldor, Melkor's commitment to defeat the Elves which is repeated in Sauron's desire to control them. The Flame Imperishable manifests itself countless times in the nature of Arda; however, it comes to life in real terms through the Two Trees, and creates the stories in *The Silmarillion*.

At this point, the existence of the Two Trees is exceptionally important, not only do they definitely belong to nature but also they are not like the other trees in Arda—they are created in an artistic way and designed in a unique fashion. This combination of nature and art is so powerful that it repeats itself many times once the chain of White Tree begins: "And since of all things in Valinor they loved most the White Tree, Yavanna made for them a tree like to a lesser image of Telperion" (ibid., 59). And the image of the White Tree extends across Aman to symbolise and comprise the whole nature of Arda. As Catherine Madsen suggests, "Middle-earth is a monotheistic world—remotely; it has no theology, no covenant, and no religious instruction; it is full of beauty and wonder and even holiness, but not divinity. Even the reader need not worship anything to comprehend it. It is more important for the reader to love trees" (Madsen, 39).

As mentioned in the first paragraph, particularly the arts and crafts of the Elves in Arda contribute to the empowerment of Arda's nature on a significant level. According to Michael Drout, the main reason behind this is the characteristics of the Elves and their unique relationship with nature surrounding them:

> This ability to work with nature without dominating it, to generate a landscape that is natural but has also been shaped and improved, is a key characteristic of the Elves and illustrates

24

how Tolkien saw them as taking the noblest and most mystical attributes of human beauty and extending them still further (Drout, 145).

So it comes as no surprise that it is Fëanor, perhaps the most skilful Elf, who adds to the artfulness of the Two Trees by creating the Silmarils from the earth of Arda but also from the light of the Trees: "And the inner fire of the Silmarils Fëanor made of the blended light of the Trees of Valinor" (*Silmarillion*, 67). The "Flame" Imperishable is the "light" of the Two Trees, which is the inner "fire" of the Silmarils. And "though the Trees have long withered and shine no more", their light stays with the Silmarils. The Flame Imperishable claims the right to continue revealing itself through the survival of Arda's nature, and through the Silmarils, the creative power in the nature of Arda manifests itself to the point that though two Silmarils are lost, one is "set to sail in the seas of heaven", thus even surpassing the boundaries of this nature. "And thus it came to pass that the Silmarils found their long homes: one in the airs of heaven, and one in the fires of the heart of the world, and one in the deep waters" (ibid., 250, 254). Like the Valar representing, spiritualising and hallowing different elements in Arda's nature, with the Silmarils the emphasis is again on the different facets of this nature.

As Verlyn Flieger suggests on the spread of the Flame Imperishable in Arda:

... his [Tolkien's] treatment lends itself increasingly to the playing out of Barfield's division of 'to shine' into spiritual reality and physical light ... his sequence begins with the pervasive light of the Lamps, continues with the softer pulsating and cyclical light of the Trees, and culminates in the Silmarils, the three great jewels made with the light of the Trees that hold the last of the light when the Trees are killed. Their resting places, the 'long home' of each in earth, sea, and sky, place the light beyond the reach of Middle-earth. The last of the light, the star Eärendil, which is the only Silmaril remaining above ground, appears to the sight of those in Middle-earth at morning and at evening, times of changing light. No longer a pervasive presence, the light has become only a reminder and a promise, a sign of what was and what yet may be (Flieger, 97 – 98).

In my understanding, in addition to being about the fate of "light" in the physical realms of both the Primary and the secondary world, thus also being one of the major elements in the inner consistency of this secondary world, the spread of the Flame Imperishable is actually its revelation and claim for its probable boundaries. As it reaches out from Aman to Middle-earth and from there to the skies, it surrounds and comprises the whole nature of Arda and naturally diminishes in the meantime. Although there is no apparent light captured to be seen, the same flame surfaces twenty times more through the Rings of Power, the main reason for the whole plot of *The Lord of the Rings*. The Rings are all made from the very earth of Arda. Through the repetition and inescapability of its power of creation, the nature of Arda always subsists to lay claim to this secondary world. It is alive, full of spirit and endless potential, and reminds the reader of it throughout the entire mythology.

At this point, there could also be drawn an analogy between neo-pagan religions in the Primary World and the philosophies of some specific characters in the secondary one. The prominent characteristic of neo-pagan religions is that they approach nature in terms of art and philosophy. Their philosophical understanding of death and immortality of human soul is similar to the reasons for some characters in Arda to practice art as a tribute to nature's glory. Yavanna is aware of the fact that Arda will always be the main creation and labour of the Valar, and also remain as their home at least until the Second Music; therefore she makes the Two Trees "awake" as a symbol of nature's awakening. Fëanor cannot be satisfied with the mere existence of the Two Trees as the icon of the light of nature, and seeks a more secure way of proving the power of nature; he "… pondered how the light of the Trees, the glory of the Blessed Realm, might be preserved imperishable" (*Silmarillion*, 67). At this point, our encounter with the same word, "imperishable", is almost a proof that Fëanor creates the Silmarils to manifest the Flame Imperishable, which has been revealed by the Two Trees before in the form of light and is actually "the glory of the Blessed Realm". Since the glory of Aman is this imperishable flame and this blessed realm sets an example for the rest of Arda as for spreading the practice of art, it means that this same Secret Fire is actually the power of creativity hidden in the nature of Arda in general. Fëanor has a certain level of philosophical understanding about the creative power of nature and how the immortality of their souls depends on it via the existence of the Halls of Mandos, and practices the art of Silmarils to continue this artistry. It is almost like he has a spiritual responsibility to carry out this practice as a denizen of this nature.

What Melian achieves under the name of the Girdle of Melian is to use nature's protection to protect a certain part of nature itself. The Girdle is built upon the forests surrounding the realm of Doriath to keep this kingdom safe from the evil forces of Melkor. It is an obvious attribution to the enduring spirit of nature. The Girdle is lifted after a long time but this never means a failure in terms of nature, on the contrary, the time comes for Arda's nature to renew itself and perhaps by sensing this in the depths of her heart and mind, Melian abandons Beleriand. A thousand years later, in another age, the Rings of Power start to be forged under the leadership of Celebrimbor. The word "power" is related more to magic and evil rather than art and good in Tolkien's secondary world, and their different contexts are demarcated clearly many times by Tolkien. From the aspect of the whole journey of the Rings, however, power may be interpreted in numerous ways, and this paper aims to point at the origins of it, which is the nature of Arda. The Rings are like the fruits granted by Mother Nature through the creative minds and hands of the Elven smiths of Eregion. Therefore, they are the signs showing that nature has not been ended yet; it still has that creativeness in earth for those who are capable of realizing and evaluating it. Immortal spirit of nature is revealed again through the immortality of the Elves, but to be lost again. Two ages and more than two thousand years after Melian abandons Beleriand, Galadriel leaves Middle-earth with Nenya, and the long protected Lothlórien is left to decay.

What happens afterwards in terms of nature is not certain, but the readers have already been given numerous clues about its creative power that the nature of Arda will be alive as long as this secondary world exists. As for *The Lord of the Rings*, Tolkien wrote in one of his letters:

The only criticism that annoyed me was one that it 'contained no religion' (and 'no Women', but that does not matter, and is not true anyway). It is a monotheistic world of 'natural theology'. The odd fact that there are no churches, temples, or religious rites and ceremonies, is simply part of the historical climate depicted … I am in any case myself a Christian; but the 'Third Age' was not a Christian world (*Letters*, 220).

The concept of natural theology can be found even more strongly in the First and Second Age revealed in *The Silmarillion*. However, it is important to highlight that only imagination, and using this power to see and create art from nature can enable the readers to see the existence of a common belief in nature shared by different creatures in Arda. As William Blake wrote in one of his letters to the Reverend John Trusler: "The tree which moves some to tears of joy is in the Eyes of others only a Green thing that stands in the way. Some See Nature all Ridicule and Deformity & by these I shall not regulate my proportions, & Some Scarce see Nature at all[.] But to the Eyes of the Man of Imagination Nature is Imagination itself[.]" The whole mythology gathers around Arda's inner spirit, the Ainur sing for the sake of Arda's physical existence and its denizens thread along its forests and through its mountains hallowing Arda's nature and creating many artworks inspired by the earth.

Bibliography

Bentley, G.E. *William Blake's Writings*. Clarendon Press, 1978.

Drout, Michael D.C. "Eldamar", in *J. R. R. Tolkien Encyclopedia*. Routledge, 2007.

Flieger, Verlyn. *Splintered Light: Logos and Language in Tolkien's World*. The Kent State University Press, 2002.

Madsen, Catherine. "'Light from an Invisible Lamp': Natural Religion in The Lord of the Rings." *Tolkien and the Invention of Myth*. Edited by Jane Chance, The University Press of Kentucky, 2004, pp. 35-47.

Tolkien, J. R.R. *The Letters of J.R.R. Tolkien*. Edited by Humphrey Carpenter with the assistance of Christopher Tolkien, Harper Collins Publishers, 2006.

---. *The Silmarillion*. Houghton Mifflin Harcourt, 2001.

Honouring the Valar, Seeking the Elf Within: The Curious History of Tolkien Spirituality and the Religious Affordance of Tolkien's Literary Mythology

Markus Altena Davidsen

In Tolkien Studies, much has been written about the religious and mythological sources that Tolkien worked into his own literary mythology, and it is heatedly debated what Tolkien's stories and letters reveal about his own personal beliefs. Was Tolkien a full-blooded Catholic? Or did he also have Pagan sympathies? Did he believe in ancestral memory, and in Faery? The topic of my talk is different, though. I will be discussing a phenomenon that I call Tolkien spirituality. By this term I refer to groups and individuals who, since the 1960s, have developed increasingly sophisticated religious beliefs, practices, and traditions based on Tolkien's literary mythology.

Tolkien spirituality is a form of religion, but it is does not constitute a religious movement in the conventional sense. There is no central leadership, various groups have emerged independently of each other, and many individuals involved in Tolkien spirituality are not even member of any organised group. What we have, then, are Tolkien fans with a religious background as Christians, Neo-Pagans, or religious seekers, who at one point began to fuse their religious engagement with their engagement in Tolkien fandom. Most of these individuals continue to be 'just Tolkien fans' (they love the books, and some learn the Elven languages) and they continue to be 'just Christians' or 'just Pagans' (and hence attend church or venerate the ancient gods and goddesses). But in addition to this, they perform rituals that honour the Valar (and occasionally also the Elves and Eru) and/or entertain the belief that they are in some way Elves themselves. It is difficult so say how big the community is because most of those involved in Tolkien spirituality practice alone and are difficult to locate. My best guess is that those currently affiliated with a group devoted exclusively or partly to Tolkien spirituality should be counted in the hundreds.

I wrote my PhD dissertation on Tolkien spirituality (Davidsen 2014), and I am now working hard to finish a thoroughly rewritten market edition (Davidsen fc.).[1] If all goes well, the book will come out in 2020, and will be published open access. In this lecture I will present a few of the results from my research into Tolkien spirituality. Indeed I will do two things. First, I will offer a sketch of the history of Tolkien spirituality from the hippies in the late 1960s till today's online groups. Second, I will raise the question why a religious milieu could emerge that uses Tolkien's literary mythology as its central text. I will argue that it is because Tolkien's stories imitate the rhetoric of real religious narratives and therefore affords a religious reading (cf. Davidsen 2016).

---

1. This lecture draws on these published and forthcoming works and therefore includes only a minimal amount of references. Please consult my doctoral dissertation (online accessible and searchable) for further details and references.

The Curious History of Tolkien Spirituality

It all began when *The Lord of the Rings* appeared as affordable paperback in the United States and the United Kingdom in 1965. The hippies took Tolkien to heart, and *The Lord of the Rings* outsold the Bible in the United States in 1967 and 1968 (Helms 1987, 105). Hippies married in ceremonies based on the book and read passages from it during LSD-trips to amplify the spiritual experience (Ratliff and Flinn 1968, 144). Especially the chapter on the Fellowship's stay in dreamlike Lothlórien was reported to deepen the spiritual experience. At the same time, some of Tolkien's readers wondered whether The Lord of the Rings was in fact a parable about Faery and joined the emerging Neo-Pagan movement to explore the Celtic and Germanic mythologies from which Tolkien had drawn much of his inspiration. As Graham Harvey has explained, Tolkien's works provided the "metaphorical bino¬culars through which the realm of Faerie became visible again" (2000).

The first group that took *The Lord of the Rings* quite literally was active in the Mojave Desert around 1973 (Ellwood 2002, 133; cf. Davidsen 2014, 202-203). The leader, Myrtle Reece, claimed to be in contact with Bilbo, and the group believed that Middle-earth was our world in ancient prehistory and hoped to dig up Minas Tirith in the Mojave Desert. Unfortunately, the date set for the excavations continued to be postponed, and the group fell apart.

In the 1970s emerged also the movement of self-identified Elves. It began when two American magicians, known as Arwen and Elanor, allegedly were told by an Ouija board spirit to found a feminist, Elven, magical group and call it "The Elf Queen's Daughters" – the Elf Queen being a reference to

Elbereth, the Star Queen. Arwen and Elanor 'awakened' many other Elves and wrote about 300 letters of Elf Magic Mail that were distributed among the growing community and in many cases published in mainstream Neo-Pagan magazines, such as *Green Egg*. Inspiration from Tolkien was evident in this group: each member took a Tolkienesque Elven name, and Elbereth hymns from *The Lord of the Rings* were used in ritual. On the other hand, the use of Tolkien was quite liberal: The group equated Elbereth /Varda with Arda or Mother Earth, and considered anyone who took proper care of our planet to be an Elf in a metaphorical sense. The very self-identification as Elves was thus metaphorical and quite tongue-in-cheek, but Arwen and Elanor awakened others who were to take their Elven identity more seriously. The most important of these second-generation Elves were Zardoa Love and Silverflame, together the Silver Elves, who since the 1980s took over the role as the Elven movement's chief intellectuals.

Shortly after Zardoa had been awakened, *The Silmarillion* was published, and the wealth of information within this book about the culture and religion of the Elves was a true gift to the emerging Elven movement. Had that book not been published, the Elven movement had probably died out with when Arwen and Elanor stopped their letter writing and formed the Elven rock band Aeron instead. Now it offered the Silver Elves, as well as many other awakened Elves, a means to consolidate their Elven identity. And indeed, in the first decade or so, Tolkien was absolutely central to the Elven movement. The Silver Elves told me, however, that they did not attempt to re-enact Tolkien's mythology *en bloc*. Instead, they used his books "as emotive guidelines for creating [their] own Elven Culture". For example, it was Tolkien's invented languages that had inspired them to create their own 30,000 words language called Arvyndase (or Silver¬speech).

To this day, the Elven Community struggles with its Tolkienesque roots. A minority believes to be Quendi – at least to some degree. The majority, however, asserts that Tolkien's works are fiction, that only wannabes believe to be Quendi, and that serious Elves identify with the elves of folklore and mythology. Even for the majority, however, Tolkien's influence (and later Jackson's) is clearly visible, for example, in members' artwork and in their descriptions of visions of the Elven world.

The new information on the Elves and the Valar in *The Silmarillion* not only facilitated the consolidation of the Elven movement. It also enabled the emergence of a new generation of successful and seriously Tolkien-inspired religious groups for whom ritual interaction with the Valar was the central element. The largest of these groups is the Tribunal of the Sidhe, which was founded in 1984 in Sacramento, California, and is still active today. The group consists of about twenty local circles, including a Circle of the Quendi, and at least one of these is now led by second-generation members. In essence, the Tribunal of the Sidhe is a Neo-Pagan organization, and like many other Pagan groups they venerate gods and goddesses from different pantheons, especially the Celtic and Germanic. In addition to this, however, they also perform rituals directed at the Valar, especially the fertility Valië Yavanna.

Furthermore, members believe to be Changelings, that is elves, but also satyrs, fairies, and so on, who hail from an astral home-world. This idea draws on a motif from *The Lost Tales*, namely that the Valar entered Eä with a large entourage of lesser spirits. Most members of the Tribunal believe to be reincarnations of these lesser spirits rather than of the Quendi

35

(though the border between these two classes of beings is not drawn very sharply). As an extra corollary, the group claims to have established with magical research that Tolkien was a "Bard of the kin folk", i.e. that he was a Changeling himself who chose to be incarnated in a human body to tell the truth of the Changelings in fictional form.

The Silmarillion also inspired occultists of various sorts to construct Tolkien-based rituals. In 1990, Gareth Knight, a famous British occultist, published *The Magical World of the Inklings* in which he claimed that Tolkien had obtained secret knowledge from the so-called akashic records – the place where all spiritual knowledge is stored according to Theosophy – and that he had worked this secret knowledge into his books (Knight 1990, 130). The book also included a very elaborate visualization ritual composed by Vivienne Jones, "The Voyage West", in which four humans, the Elf Glorfindel, and Melian the Maia sail by "the Straight Road" to Tol Eressëa where they are welcomed by Queen Galadriel. There, they make a "Rainbow Bridge" through which healing energy can flow into Middle-earth. A few years later, in North Carolina, Vincent Bridges of the Fifth Way Mystery School constructed a "High Elvish Working", based on the pentagram rituals used by ceremonial magicians. This ritual was performed at various pagan festivals, circulated in print among pagans in the United States and New Zealand, and was later published online. Both of these rituals inspired the rituals of later Tolkien spirituality groups.

It is also worth mentioning that the British Tarot deck developer Terry Donaldson published *The Lord of the Rings* Tarot in 1997. The deck uses the standard Rider-Waite system, but depicts characters and scenes from *The Lord of the Rings* and *The Hobbit*. For example, the card Death shows Gandalf confronting the Balrog of Moria. The deck can be bought with a manual that offers a deeper description of the meaning of each card, takes account of *The Silmarillion*, and legitimizes the use of Tolkien's mythology as the basis of a tarot deck. As Donaldson puts it, it would be "missing the point" to read Tolkien's works as "a fairy story", for "Tolkien's work was in reality a monumental act of channelling".

Peter Jackson's movie adaptation of *The Lord of the Rings* led to a new wave of Tolkien spirituality, this time on the Internet. A central initiative in this respect was the Alternative Tolkien Society, a smial of the Tolkien Society that was active between 1996 and 2005. Several of the articles in *Reunion*, the online journal of the Alternative Tolkien Society, dealt with visiting Middle-earth in pathworking rituals or described experiences that may have been encounters with elves. Furthermore, several of the individuals who founded groups that were more explicitly into Tolkien spirituality had first subscribed to *Reunion*. It was also Martin Baker, the editor of *Reunion*, who introduced Calantirniel and Nathan Elwin, the two founders of Tië eldaliéva (Quenya: The Elven Path) to each other.

Tië eldaliéva (f. 2005), and its offshoot Ilsaluntë Valion (Qenya: The Silver Ship of the Valar; f. 2007), are interesting because they belong to a new type of groups that have attempted, as loyally as possible, to reconstruct the spiritual traditions of the elves (or humans) of Middle-earth. Members of these groups study Tolkien's letters as well as core texts in *The History of Middle-earth*, especially the two aborted but seemingly autobiographical "time-travel" stories, "The Lost Road" and "The Notion Club Papers", that stage Middle-earth as our world in prehistory. Based on diligent studies of Tolkien's texts, members have also reconstructed an elven ritual calendar consisting of six solar and thirteen lunar observances and developed an elaborate correspondence system. However, as Tolkien's Legendarium includes no descriptions of actual rituals, the group's ritual format has been inspired by ceremonial magic in the tradition of the Hermetic Order of the Golden Dawn and Wicca, and by neo-shamanism (Davidsen 2017). Members also draw on various esoteric concepts to make sense of their theology and cosmology (e.g., Jung's archetypes; Corbin's notion of the Imaginal Realm; cf. Davidsen 2014, 410-426).

Some Conclusions So Far

Now that we have gone through the history of Tolkien spirituality, it is possible to draw a few conclusions about what kind of religious practice Tolkien spirituality is in general. It is useful to draw these conclusions before raising the issue of the religious affordance of Tolkien's literary mythology.

Firstly, all people involved in Tolkien spirituality insist that Tolkien's stories about Middle-earth are more than fiction – that they include a spiritual truth that Tolkien intended his readers to look for. In many cases this assertion is backed up with the claim that Tolkien had based his books on some kind of revelation experience.

Secondly, people involved in Tolkien spirituality craft rituals in which they engage with Tolkien's world. These rituals come in two main forms. Either the practitioners imagine themselves travelling to Middle-earth or the Blessed Realm in trance. Or they invoke the deities of Tolkien's world (especially the Valar) to come visit them in this world. In the online age, some groups have carried out these rituals using Skype.

Thirdly, certain beliefs undergird those rituals, namely that Middle-earth and the Blessed Realm are in some way real places – perhaps existing on a spiritual plane, and that the superhuman beings from Tolkien's cosmology (especially the Valar, but also the Elves, Eru, and Gandalf) exist and deeply care about humans here on earth. Only a minority consider Tolkien's stories to be reliable historiography. And for all of them, the experience of having contact with the Valar and the Elves is more important than the question whether the War of the Ring really happened.

Finally, most practitioners of Tolkien spirituality are also strongly fascinated by the Elves, and some even go so far as to claim to *be* Elves themselves. Some of these self-identified Elves claim to possess some portion of Elven genes, pointing out that Elves and humans can procreate and that Elven genes entered the human gene pool, for example with Arwen. More often, however, the self-identified Elves claim to possess an Elven soul or spirit, claiming that Elves reincarnate and that sometimes this goes wrong with the result that an Elven soul ends up in a human body. It is for this reason, the self-identified Elves argue, that they don't really feel at home among the humans (almost muggles), but long to return to their Elven homeworld.

In addition, two patterns can be discerned in the development of Tolkien spirituality over the decades (cf. Davidsen 2012). Firstly, practitioners of Tolkien spirituality have come to ascribe more and more reality to Tolkien's world over the years. The hippies and pagans mainly played with Tolkien. By contrast, in the 21st century online groups, the reality of Tolkien's world and its inhabitant is simply taken for granted. One of my informants even told me that she considered the

Valar to be the real archetypal beings whom humans had given different names in their various mythologies. Of course this interpretation echoes the Elf Lindo in *The Lost Tales*.

We also see that new groups have emerged over time for whom Tolkien's works become increasingly central. Initially, Tolkien spirituality was something that was added to another, more fundamental, practice: The Elf Queen's Daughters were magicians, the Tribunal of the Sidhe were Pagans, and so on. Only in the 21st century, do we see groups that aim to develop traditions based exclusively on Tolkien.

I think these patterns can easily be explained. The emergence of the Internet made it possible for individuals with very peculiar interests (such as developing Tolkien-true spiritual traditions) to find each other and develop communities. In addition, the publication of first *The Silmarillion* and later *The History of Middle-earth* offered spiritual Tolkien groups an increasingly rich textual corpus to work with – indeed one of such scope and complexity that it could serve as the chief textual foundation for a new tradition, which *The Lord of the Rings* alone could not.

The Religious Affordance of Tolkien's Literary Mythology

So Tolkien spirituality exists. It is out there. This immediately raises the question 'how is that possible?' Why is there such as thing as spirituality based on Tolkien's literary mythology, when there is no, say, *A Game of Thrones* spirituality? I think that the crucial difference between Tolkien's literary mythology and *A Game of Thrones* is not one of content. Tolkien's narratives feature deities who interfere in the affairs of world, prophecies that come true, and sages (esp. Gandalf) who gives lectures on theology. But that is no different in *A Game of Thrones*: here are also gods, magic, and visions in abundance. The difference lies instead, I think, in textual form or rhetorical strategy. While Tolkien's stories do not outright claim to be non-fictional, they certainly cast doubt on their fictional status in a lot of ways, while *A Game of Thrones* does no such thing. It is because of this that Tolkien's literary mythology affords religious use, whereas *A Game of Thrones* does not.

In my article "The Religious Affordance of Supernatural Fiction: A Semiotic Approach" (Davidsen 2016), I have identified a number of veracity mechanisms that religious narratives use to construct an aura of factuality around the supernatural elements in the story-world. There is no room to go into details here (consult Davidsen 2016 for those), but the big point is that Tolkien's literary mythology has ten of these eleven mechanisms whereas *A Game of Thrones* has none. Most of these veracity mechanism are found in (the frame story of) *The Lord of the Rings*, and the rest is supplied by certain core texts in a *History of Middle-earth*, including "The Lost Road" and "The Notion Club Papers", together with Tolkien's letters. *The Silmarillion* does not explicitly thematise its own veracity, but is an unmissable text nonetheless because it supplies most of the information on the religion of the Elves. In essence, it is the veracity mechanisms of the frame story in *The Lord of the Rings* and the theological and cosmological content of *The Silmarillion* that does the trick. Since I cannot go through all veracity mechanisms, I will limit the discussion to two mechanisms that are particularly pronounced in Tolkien's narratives.

One of these veracity mechanisms is author-narrator conflation. This is probably the most effective veracity mechanism, and that is because fiction usually maintains a very clear boundary between the text-external author and the text-internal narrator. Indeed, such as 'author-narrator disjunction' is a conventional 'signpost of fictionality'. As author-narrator disjunction signals fictionality, author-narrator conflation signals non-fictionality. *The Lord of the Rings* has elements of author-narrator conflation, especially in the prologue and the appendices. The narrator of *The Lord of the Rings* is clearly a scholar, indeed a scholar of ancient history and languages. He is also human. Addressing the reader, he says that the Hobbits refer to "us" as "The Big Folk", and he compares the calendar of the Elves in Middle-earth with "our" Gregorian calendar. In short: the narrator is very much like Tolkien, and this can leave the reader wonder whether the narrative is really fact disguised as fiction, rather than fiction disguised as fact.

In the foreword to the first edition of *The Fellowship of the Ring* Tolkien went even further. He thanks his friends and family for support (as author), but he also ensures the reader that the map of the Shire included in the book has "been approved as reasonably correct by those Hobbits that still concern themselves with ancient history" (1954, 8). Here is no disjunction between Tolkien-the-author and the narrator of the story; the two are completely conflated. The original prologue can therefore be read as Tolkien's serious claim that hobbits still exist and have assisted in publishing the book. It has been reported that some lending libraries in Britain read the prologue in this manner and classified the book, at least initially, as history rather than fiction.

The conflation of author and narrator, together with the frame narrative of Bilbo and Frodo writing the story, the presentation of the Valar and Elves as real beings within the narrative world, and many other mechanisms, contributes to creating an effect of factuality. Tolkien of course did all of this tongue-in-cheek and used the expression "feigned history" about his work. The interesting thing is that while most readers, including most practitioners of Tolkien spirituality, do not read *The Lord of the Rings* as accurate history, the 'factuality effect' created by the feigned history ploy still affects them. It leaves a vague idea in many readers of 'there must be something more to it' or 'Tolkien must have done this for a reason'.

Also Tolkien's letters include passages that ascribe veracity to his narratives. It is well-known that Tolkien had the experience of not creating his world, but of merely "recording" or "reporting" what was already there. Or, as he says in another letter, "[the tales] arose in my mind as given things" (Tolkien 1981, 145). In yet another letter he even speculates that he might be a "chosen instrument" (Tolkien 1981, 431), through whom certain eternal values have been revealed. Members of Tolkien spirituality use these passages to argue that Tolkien's narratives are in fact based on revelation: that they stem from a divine source that guarantees their authority and truth. As they see it Tolkien had a revelation, and he knew it. His books describe the spiritual world that he had been in contact with. And it was his intention that people should use his books to get in touch with that very same spiritual reality. That is, practitioners of Tolkien spirituality say that it is Tolkien's normal readers who get him wrong – those who read his works as mere fiction. It is the practitioners of Tolkien spirituality who use Tolkien's books as he himself intended them to be used. While we may find such a reading far-fetched, we must admit that Tolkien's own words make such a reading possible. In other words, Tolkien's narratives have religious affordance, because Tolkien himself cast doubt on their status as just fiction.

Bibliography

Davidsen, Markus Altena. "The Spiritual Milieu Based on J.R.R. Tolkien's Literary Mythology." *Handbook of Hyper-real Religions.* Edited by A. Possamai, Brill, 2012, pp. 185 – 204.

---. "The Spiritual Tolkien Milieu: A Study of Fiction-based Religion", doctoral diss., Leiden University, 2014. Full-text available at https://openaccess.leidenuniv.nl/handle/1887/29078. (Accessed 1-Jul-2018).

---. "The Elven Path and the Silver Ship of the Valar: Two Spiritual Groups Based on J. R. R. Tolkien's Legendarium", including two appendices, "Tië eldaliéva", by Rev. Michaele Alyras de Cygne and Calantirniel, and "Ilsaluntë Valion". *Fiction, Invention and Hyper-reality: From Popular Culture to Religion.* Edited by C.M. Cusack and P. Kosnáč Routledge, 2017, pp. 15 – 39.

---. *Tolkien Spirituality: Constructing Belief and Tradition in Fiction-based Religion.* De Gruyter, forthcoming.

Ellwood, Robert S. 2002. *Frodo's Quest: Living the Myth in The Lord of the Rings.* Wheaton, Illinois: Quest Books: The Theosophical Publishing House.

Harvey, Graham. 2000. "Fantasy in the Study of Religions: Paganism as Observed and Enhanced by Terry Pratchett". *Diskus* (now *Journal of the British Association for the Study of Religion*) 6. http://jbasr.com/basr/diskus/diskus1-6/harvey-6.txt. (Accessed 1-Jul-2018).

Helms, Philips W. "The Evolution of Tolkien Fandom", *A Tolkien Treasury.* Edited by A. Becker, Courage Books, 2000, pp. 104 – 109.

Knight, Gareth [Basil Wilby]. *The Magical World of the Inklings.* Element Books, 1990.

Ratliff, William E. and Charles G. Flinn. "The Hobbit and the Hippie." *Modern Age*, vol. 12, 1968, pp. 142-146.

Tolkien, J. R. R. "Foreword." *The Fellowship of the Ring, Being the First Part of The Lord of the Rings*, George Allen & Unwin, 1954, pp. 7 – 8.

---. *The Letters of J.R.R. Tolkien*. Edited by Humphrey Carpenter with the assistance of Christopher Tolkien, George Allen & Unwin, 1981.

Tolkien's Mandos, Pratchett's Death

Justin Lewis-Anthony

"Tolkien's Dead" – Pratchett's debt to Tolkien

"Tolkien's dead. JK Rowling said no. Philip Pullman couldn't make it. Hi, I'm Terry Pratchett."

Terry Pratchett's admiration of, and debt to, J.R.R. Tolkien was clear from the moment that the young Terence wrote a fan letter to the Professor about *Smith of Wotton Major* (Pratchett, 'Letter to J.R.R. Tolkien (22 November 1967)'). Pratchett admitted his debt all through his professional life[1], and, when he became a wildly successful author himself, took to wearing to fan conventions a t-shirt with greeting reproduced above (Pratchett and Kidby). It managed to be both modest ("I'm the best last choice"), and slyly boastful ("Of course I'm counted amongst these luminaries").

---

1. When asked by *The New York Times* for his favourite fantasy novelists: O.K., I give in. J. R. R. Tolkien. I wrote a letter to him once and got a very nice reply. Just think how busy he would have been, and yet he took the time out to write to a fan. ('By The Book')

As he said in another place:

I just said that I'd enjoyed the book very much. And he said thank you. For a moment, it achieved the most basic and treasured of human communications: you are real, and therefore so am I. (Pratchett, 'Kevins' 104)

It is curious, and significant, that Pratchett claimed the link to Tolkien through the latter's death. One of the central themes of Tolkien's legendarium is death and immortality (Letter 186 (to Joanna de Bortadano), *Letters*). In Pratchett's Discworld cycle one of the central characters and themes is Death, and his interactions with humanity and creation. Death became such an important part of Pratchett's legendarium that it was Death himself who announced Pratchett's own death on 12 March 2015 in a series of tweets, after the author had lived with posterior cortical atrophy (PCA), a form of Alzheimer's disease.[2]

Pratchett's writing was, in part, a reaction to Tolkien, so what similarities and differences can we see in the ways in which the two treat death and its (his?) consequences. In doing so, we have to bear in mind the judgment of Death's own adopted daughter, Susan Sto Helit, that it is "frankly…quite ridiculous to go anthropomorphizing a simple natural function…"? (*Soul Music*, 85).[3]

---

2. "AT LAST, SIR TERRY, WE MUST WALK TOGETHER."

Terry took Death's arm and followed him through the doors and on to the black desert under the endless night.

The End.

(Pratchett, 'AT LAST, SIR TERRY, WE MUST WALK TOGETHER.'; Pratchett, 'Terry Took Death's Arm and Followed Him through the Doors and on to the Black Desert under the Endless Night.'; Pratchett, 'The End.')

3. Quoting from Pratchett's work is problematic, in that there is (yet!) no critical edition, each book has been published in multiple versions, and he, famously, did not write in chapters (so the critic is unable to refer, Tolkien-style, to, for example, TT.3.VI, indicating *The Two Towers*, book 3, chapter 6). The best one can do is refer to the page number of the edition cited in the bibliography and hope for the speedy arrival of a uniform critical and annotated edition.

Anthropomorphizing a Simple Natural Function

In order to tease out the connections, I propose that we look at Death and death, under the Sto Helit categories: how do our authors treat death as the natural function that marks the ending of conscious life? How do our authors then anthropomorphise that natural function, and what does it say about the cosmologies at play?

Curiously, the attention that the two authors pay to these two categories are almost exactly and inversely proportioned. Tolkien, a devout Catholic, for whom the whole of his legendarium was written under, and influenced by his Christian faith, pays very little attention to the anthropomorphising of death: to a large extent, death is not a character in a cosmos in which many natural and supernatural phenomena become characters. On the other hand, Pratchett, the humanist atheist who has produced some of the most cogent and effective criticisms against religious or non-material world-views, is unable to describe the death of a character, without introducing a non-material and supranatural being. Death becomes Terry.

Mandos and Death

This is not to say that Tolkien's cosmos lacks a death figure. As we find in 'Valaquenta' Tolkien includes a lord of the dead, if not a lord of Death. Mandos, who is properly called Námo, is the "keeper of the Houses of the Dead" and the "summoner of the spirits of the slain." He is the record keeper of creation: 'he forgets nothing; and he knows all things that shall be.' He is also the "Doomsman of the Valar"; but, unlike Pratchett's Death, who often has disturbingly freelance tendencies, 'he pronounces his dooms and his judgements only at the bidding of Manwë.' He is espoused to Vairë the Weaver, while Pratchett's Death is heartbreakingly alone (*Silmarillion*, 28).

Mandos is grim; the grimness comes with the job. But he is not implacable. When Beren dies, Lúthien comes to the halls of Mandos and sings a song of grief and pleading before him, a song that is the 'most fair that ever in words was woven, and the song most sorrowful that ever the world shall hear.' All the Valar are moved by the memory of it, and Mandos, who heard it first is 'moved to pity, who never before was so moved, nor has been since' ('Of Beren and Lúthien', *Silmarillion*, chap. 19).

Death, on the other hand, may be equally grim. He always speaks in SMALL CAPS. Death greets all significant travellers on the journey from life to what comes next.[4] In *Mort*, where Death takes on an apprentice, it is a moment of maturity when the apprentice realises good people die, bad things happen, bad people thrive: "There's no justice," he cries. Death sighs and replies: "NO. THERE IS NO JUSTICE. THERE'S JUST ME" (*Mort*, 49). Over the arc of the Discworld mythos, his character develops to the extent that he is angered by injustice, and cruelty to cats, and his greatest enemies are not evil humans, but the Auditors of Reality, the supranatural beings who regard life as making the cosmos untidy. In *Reaper Man*, while on holiday from his day job, Death, travelling under the pseudonym of Bill Door, saves a little girl from dying in a fire:

---

4. Of course, it is interesting to test what counts as "significance"? As one of my correspondents has pointed out, there is a hint of works-righteousness in Pratchett's atheism: important people receive the important psychopomp, but who is to determine "importance"?

Death knew that to tinker with the fate of one individual could destroy the whole world. He knew this. The knowledge was built into him.

To Bill Door, he realised, it was so much horse elbows.

OH, DAMN, he said. And walked into the fire (*Reaper Man* 138).

Who is Death calling upon here, when he calls damnation down upon his situation? Who is the authority to determine damnation and salvation when there is no mercy, there is no justice, there is only Death?

Death might be an implacable anthropomorphic force, but he's on the side of the little person against the bosses: especially if the bosses are the Auditors of Reality. The consequences of saving the girl's life, or, rather, preventing her death from occurring at the proper time, requires Bill Door/Death to appear before the demiurge of Discworld

"ALL THINGS THAT ARE, ARE OURS. BUT WE MUST CARE. FOR IF WE DO NOT CARE, WE DO NOT EXIST. IF WE DO NOT EXIST, THEN THERE IS NOTHING BUT BLIND OBLIVION. AND EVEN OBLIVION MUST END SOMEDAY. LORD, WILL YOU GRANT ME JUST A LITTLE TIME? FOR THE PROPER BALANCE OF THINGS. TO RETURN WHAT WAS GIVEN. FOR THE SAKE OF PRISONERS AND THE FLIGHT OF BIRDS.

Death took a step backwards. It was impossible to read expression in Azrael's features. Death glanced sideways at the servants.

LORD, WHAT CAN THE HARVEST HOPE FOR, IF NOT FOR THE CARE OF THE REAPER MAN?" (*Reaper Man* 264)

And when Death experiences the possibility of death, he finds the experience almost overwhelming:

Was that what it was really like to be alive? The feeling of darkness dragging you forward?

How could they live with it? And yet they did, and even seemed to find enjoyment in it, when surely the only sensible course would be to despair. Amazing. To feel you were a tiny living thing, sandwiched between two cliffs of darkness. How could they stand to be alive?

Obviously it was something you had to be born to (*Reaper Man* 127).

Where did Pratchett's idea for this Death come from? We get a clue from the first time we meet Death in Pratchett's legendarium, in the company of the anti-hero, Rincewind:

Thus it was that Rincewind, hurrying through the crowded, flare-lit evening bazaars of Morpork with the luggage trundling behind him, jostled a tall dark figure, turned to deliver a few suitable curses, and beheld Death.

It had to be Death. No-one else went around with empty eye sockets and, of course, the scythe over one shoulder was another clue. As Rincewind stared in horror a courting couple, laughing at some private joke, walked straight through the apparition without appearing to notice it.

Death, insofar as it was possible in a face with no movable features, looked surprised.

RINCEWIND? Death said, in tones as deep and heavy as the slamming of leaden doors, far underground.

...I WAS SURPRISED THAT YOU JOSTLED ME, RINCEWIND. FOR I HAVE AN APPOINTMENT WITH THEE THIS VERY NIGHT.

'Oh no, not—'
OF COURSE, WHAT'S SO BLOODY VEXING ABOUT
THE WHOLE BUSINESS IS THAT I WAS EXPECTING TO
MEET THEE IN PSEPHOPOLOLIS.
'But that's five hundred miles away!'
YOU DON'T HAVE TO TELL ME, THE WHOLE
SYSTEM'S GOT SCREWED UP AGAIN. I CAN SEE
THAT. LOOK THERE'S NO CHANCE OF YOU—? (*The
Colour of Magic* 62).

Death is peeved and peevish. He has a job to do, and
circumstances, for some unaccountable reason, are making it
harder for him to complete his job. Even anthropomorphised
natural functions have pride in their work.

This first introduction to Death is a significant one in the
Discworld canon. It tells us both of the implacability of death,
the permanent cessation of the vital functions of the living
person, and the implacability of Death, the (much beloved)
character of the Discworld universe. It is significant that
Pratchett chooses to introduce Death using the manner of a
familiar story. Rincewind's "appointment in Psephopololis" is
very clearly a parody of the parable-within-a-play, commonly
called 'Appointment in Samarra', by W. Somerset Maugham
(*Sheppey, a Play in Three Acts*; later collected in 'Sheppey'
298). Pratchett recalls his mother reading the story to him as a
small boy: "My mother told me the 'Appointment in Samarra'
story when I was very young, and it remained. She says she
read it somewhere, or maybe heard it… I'd always thought it
was from the *1001 Nights*, although I never went looking for
it. It's one of those stories that a lot of people vaguely know,

without quite knowing why…" (Breebaart and Kew 11).[5]

Death and death were familiar to Pratchett for the entirety of his adult life. As he was fond of saying, in the author's biographies printed in the Discworld books: 'He started work as a journalist one day in 1965 and saw his first corpse three hours later, work experience meaning something in those days' (which is the version printed for *Interesting Times*). The body was 'an *extremely* dead body' (Introduction to 'The King and I', Pratchett, *Slip* 223). Two years after Pratchett's death, BBC Two broadcast a programme based on his uncompleted memoirs.[6] Paul Kaye, playing Pratchett, and speaking the author's words, divulged that the poor corpse had been found in the bottom of a slurry pit (Russell). His responsibilities as a journalist included sitting in the coroners' courts of Buckinghamshire, listening to the "demise of some luckless citizen found dead in his car, in his garage with a pipe from the exhaust through a partly open window." This was a glum and dismal experience: "people find

5. A version of the story does appear in Arabian Nights, but only in a manuscript version that has yet to be translated into English. The Story of King Sabâ, Night 526 in the so-called 'Reinhardt' MS of the Arabian Nights (I:436b-468a), interpolates a number of stories of King Solomon, of which the fourth is:

One day the angel of death enters Solomon's court and looks intensely at one of his courtiers. As the man is frightened, Solomon, in accordance with the man's wish, has him transported to India in a flash. Later, the angel of death explains to Solomon why he had been so surprised to see the man in Solomon's company: God had commanded him to fetch his soul in India on that very same day. (Summary in English in Marzolph et al. 355) The story, translated into French, is in (Chraïbi 256)

6. Pratchett had wanted to complete his memoirs, as "it is always a good idea to get the lies down in print before your enemies actually print the truth." (Gilbey).

many and varied ways to end their lives abruptly, and all of them are nasty, especially for those who have to deal with the aftermath—because suicide really needs practice..." (Pratchett, 'Genuine Absent-Minded Professor', 286).

Pratchett described his encounters with death in his family: his 'paternal grandfather died in the ambulance on the way to hospital after just having cooked and eaten his own dinner at the age of 96. ...He had felt very odd, got a neighbour to ring for the doctor and stepped tidily into the ambulance and out of the world. He died on the way to the hospital—a good death if ever there was one. Except that according to my father, he did complain to the ambulance men that he hadn't had time to finish his pudding' ('Sir Terry Pratchett: Shaking Hands with Death'; later published as *Shaking Hands with Death*. Quoted here from 'Dimbleby Lecture', 336).[7] His father was ill for a year with pancreatic cancer, during which time there was an awareness, for both father and son, that they were 'marching towards the sounds of guns' (ibid., 337). In the end, it took his father a fortnight to die in the hospice, 'as a kind of collateral damage in the war between his cancer and the morphine. And in that time he stopped being him and started becoming a corpse, all be it one that moved ever so slightly from time to time' (ibid., 337–38).

It was on returning home from his father's death that

---

7. The lecture was delivered in the library of the Royal College of Physicians, and not at the Royal Society of Medicine—two different organizations and two different address. The broadcast makes that clear, and the introduction, by Rob Wilkins, to the published text in the 2015 edition confirms that, even though the text of the lecture, in both separate and collected volumes refers to the RSM.

Pratchett had a minor accident in his car, which he later thought was the first manifestation of the Posterior Cortical Atrophy (PCA), the unusual form of Alzheimer's Disease which was eventually to kill him. Pratchett became aware of the presence of death in his life, just as he had been aware of the presence of Death from boyhood:

> When I was a young boy, playing on the floor of my grandmother's front room, I glanced up at the television and saw Death, talking to a Knight and I didn't know very much about death at that point. It was the thing that happened to budgerigars and hamsters. But it was Death, with a scythe and an amiable manner. I didn't know it at the time, of course, but I had just watched a clip from Bergman's *Seventh Seal*, wherein the Knight engages in protracted dialogue, and of course the famous chess game, with the Grim Reaper who, it seemed to me, did not seem so terribly grim (Russell).

The boyhood image informed the young adult's observations and the middle-aged man's experiences. Death, as the non-negotiable experience, and Death as a protagonist, appeared in the very first Discworld book and 'has evolved in the series to be one of its most popular characters.' He is 'implacable, because that is his job', but he also seems to be kindly disposed towards humanity, 'as ephemeral as mayflies' ('Dimbleby Lecture', 335). He is, Pratchett says, 'in short, a kindly Death, cleaning up the mess that this life leaves, and opening the gate to the next one' (ibid., 336).[8]

---

8. Which, of course, implies there is a next one! (HT Pythia).

The Role of Death

In my original abstract for this paper I had intended to compare and contrast the specific deaths of specific characters in the two authors' legendariums. The necessity for that work has been (partially) negated by the recent publication of Amy Amendt-Raduege's, *The Sweet and the Bitter*. So, within the confines of a conference paper I will mention only the deaths of two characters while still attempting to sketch the underlying philosophy and theology of death.

As Amendt-Raduege points out, there is a *lot* of death in *The Lord of Rings* alone: over fifty named characters, nine of whom are "major characters" (Amendt-Raduege 190).[9] There is no surprise in that, when one realises that for Tolkien, on reflection, his story allegorises Power and Domination, but the central theme is "something much more permanent and difficult: Death and Immortality." And, the way in which Death and Immortality are experienced by, or denied by his two great protagonist races, Mankind and Elves:

> the mystery of the love of the world in the hearts of a race 'doomed' to leave and seemingly lose it; the anguish in the hearts of a race 'doomed' not to leave it, until its whole evil-aroused story is complete. (Letter 186, *Letters*, 246)

And, for Tolkien, this is most clearly exemplified in the story of Aragorn and the death of Elessar (ibid.).

---

9. That compares with Digg's calculation of 222,970 deaths in the extended edition of Peter Jackson's *The Lord of the Rings* trilogy! (Digg).

The Death of Aragorn

As Amendt-Raduege points out, the death of Aragorn, which is told outside the structure of the narrative of *LotR*, conforms almost exactly to the pattern of the *ars moriendi*, the fifteenth century handbooks on the manner of dying well (Atkinson; referenced in Amendt-Raduege 206–08): furthermore, "the passing of Aragorn is one of the most deeply moving scenes in the story" (Amendt-Raduege 600–02). Aragorn realises that his death is upon him, and that his life is completed. As a man of high Númenórean descent he is permitted to choose the time of his death, which is not the same as choosing death out of time. He tells Arwen:

> "At last, Lady Evenstar, fairest in this world, and most beloved, my world is fading. Lo! we have gathered, and we have spent, and now the time of payment draws near."

His last words to her speak of pain, but also hope:

> "…In sorrow we must go, but not in despair. Behold! we are not bound for ever to the circles of the world, and beyond them is more than memory. Farewell!" (*LotR*, 1062, 1063)

Aragorn dies as he lived: well. But he knows, unlike most of his brothers and sisters in the race of Men, that death is a doom, and not a despair. Beyond death is more than memory. But in his wisdom, and in his compassion to Arwen, he does not speculate, nor give easy comfort. Death is painful, but the pain is not the end.

We can see this attitude, this fundamental axiom, being expressed in two of Tolkien's theoretical works: *On Fairy-Stories*, and 'Athrabeth Finrod Ah Andreth'. ('On Fairy-Stories'; 'Athrabeth', 301–66)

In the latter, an almost complete late work, Tolkien dramatizes the different understanding of Elves and Mankind as to the meaning and significance of death and immortality for them. Andreth, although a wise woman, has forgotten the true origins of death for humanity, as she believes that death came "through the malice of the Lord of the Darkness whom they do not name." For the saying is "We were not made for death, nor born ever to die. Death was imposed upon us." ('Athrabeth', 309) Finrod counsels Andreth against envying Elves for their immortality, for they understand how death works, and how it has been tainted: "dying we die, and we go out to no return. Death is an uttermost end, a loss irremediable. And it is abominable; for it is also a wrong that is done to us." (ibid., 311) Even in this death, Andreth knows that some believe there is hope for humanity:

> …they say that the One will himself enter into Arda, and heal Men and all the Marring from the beginning to the end. This they say also, or they feign, is a rumour that has come down through years uncounted, even from the days of our undoing. (ibid., 321)

Finrod has named this "deeper" hope: "*Estel* we call it, that is 'trust'. It is not defeated by the ways of the world, for it does not come from experience, but from our nature and first being" (ibid., 320). And, of course, Estel is one of the given names of Aragorn.

In *On Fairy-Stories* Tolkien famously describes the "oldest and deepest desire" in fairy-stories, namely "the Escape from Death." This "Great Escape for mortal races like humanity is matched, as an inevitable pendant with the "Escape from Deathlessness" for the immortal races like Elves, for "[f]ew lessons are taught more clearly in them than the burden of that kind of immortality, or rather endless serial living..." ('On Fairy-Stories', 68).

The Death of Mistress Weatherwax

Even in the earlier Discworld books Death and the encounter with death has already become something more than a comic encounter. In *Mort*, in a passage reminiscent of Bilbo's description of his life-weariness, Goodie Hamstring greets Death's apprentice in with an elegy that is really almost an epithalamion:

> There's some things I shall miss... But it gets thin, you know. Life, I'm referring to. You can't trust your own body any more, and it's time to move on. I reckon it's about time I tried something else... (*Mort*, 82).[10]

For Tolkien, the escape from Deathlessness is the embrace of Death. For Pratchett, Goodie Hamstring demonstrates how this

10. Compare with Bilbo's complaint to Gandalf: "Why, I feel all thin, sort of stretched, if you know what I mean: like butter that has been scraped over too much bread. That can't be right. I need a change, or something." (FR I.1, *The Lord of the Rings* 32).

59

is an embrace for the mortal races.

In *The Shepherd's Crown*, the last Discworld book, Pratchett attempts to square the circle of his beloved implacable anthropomorphic personification and the agency in life and death that he advocated both for his most human characters, and in his own life. Granny Weatherwax dies: in chapter 2! But she dies accepting of the time and place: she makes preparations, including placing two pennies by the side of her bed, and amending the usual note that accompanies her consciousness-absent body from "I ATEN'T DEAD" to "I IS PROBABLY DEAD". Her death is, unlike most of her life, courteous, to those who will find her. She accepts. As Death says when he comes for Granny:

> YOU ARE TAKING THIS VERY WELL, ESME WEATHERWAX.
> 'It's an inconvenience, true enough, and I don't like it at all, but I know that you do it for everyone, Mister Death. Is there any other way?'
> NO, THERE ISN'T, I'M AFRAID. WE ARE ALL FLOATING IN THE WINDS OF TIME. BUT YOUR CANDLE, MISTRESS WEATHERWAX, WILL FLICKER FOR SOME TIME BEFORE IT GOES OUT – A LITTLE REWARD FOR A LIFE WELL LIVED. FOR I CAN SEE THE BALANCE AND YOU HAVE LEFT THE WORLD MUCH BETTER THAN YOU FOUND IT, AND IF YOU ASK ME, said Death, NOBODY COULD DO ANY BETTER THAN THAT...
> There was no light, no point of reference except for the two tiny blue pinpricks sparkling in the eye sockets of Death himself.
> 'Well, the journey was worth taking and I saw many wonderful things on the way, including you, my reliable friend. Shall we

go now?'
MADAM, WE'VE ALREADY GONE. (*Shepherd's Crown*, 38)

Such is Pratchett's depiction and ideal of euthanasia.

Conclusion: Immortality and Memory

Death (upper-case, character), and death (lower-case, phenomenon), is an inescapable part of Pratchett's world and world-view. A.S. Byatt, in a perceptive and magnanimous review of *Night Watch*, notes how close to Pratchett's heart is the fact of death:

> Like all good storytellers he writes against death, creating impossible escapes, thrilling dangers, the come-uppance of the wicked and so on. But unlike many creators of fantasy worlds he makes sure his readers know death is real, while at the same time finding ingenious devices to help us to accommodate that knowledge (Byatt; reviewing *Night Watch*).

Which sounds, in turn, like a description of the *ars moriendi,* which, according to Amendt-Raduege, is one of the functions of *The Lord of the Rings*. Tolkien and Pratchett both are interested in what it means and what it does to live with the knowledge of death. Part of that exploration comes from how the mortal, finite, creature responds to death. However, dying well is not the whole point. As Woody Allen once said, "I'm not afraid of dying: I just don't want to be there when it happens" (Bailey).

For Pratchett there is nothing knowable beyond death, and, probably nothing at all beyond death. Our lives are limited, entirely, within the *limina* of birth and death, and we are not

61

able to anticipate our births, so we anticipate our deaths. For Tolkien, writing a pre-Christian mythology but as a devoutly Christian man, there can be nothing within the world of humanity that is not experienced under and mediated by the *eucatastrophe* of the Incarnation. We live, we die, and death not ends it (Morrison and The Doors; Morrison 4).

This is not to say that Tolkien is unaffected, intellectually or emotionally, by the fact of death. After all, he is a Christian, and he would have known that the shortest verse of the Christian bible is "Jesus wept" (Jn 11:35); the *eucatastrophe* himself, weeping at the death of his friend, Lazarus. Tolkien experienced that himself, most visibly in the death of Edith:

In those days her hair was raven, her skin clear, her eyes brighter than you have seen them, and she could sing – and *dance*. But the story has gone crooked, & I am left, and I cannot plead before the inexorable Mandos (Letter 430 to Christopher Tolkien, July 1972, *Letters* 420).

However, for Pratchett, the only thing waiting for us after death is Death, and a sky, "dark and pocked with large stars", and under the sky black sand stretching into the infinite distance: "A desert. After death, a desert. The desert. No hells, yet. Perhaps there was hope" (*Small Gods* 35). But there is no hope there, no justice, no mercy, only Death.

In the end, the greatest hope that Pratchett can find, the greatest escape from death, is memory:

...no-one is finally dead until the ripples they cause in the world die away—until the clock he wound up winds down, until the wine she made has finished its ferment, until the crop they planted is harvested. The span of someone's life, they say, is only the core of their actual existence (Reaper Man 260).

In the meantime:

He reserves the elderly curmudgeon's privilege of wishing a good death on everyone, and an early one on anyone who disagrees with him (Penny).

Bibliography

Amendt-Raduege, Amy. *The Sweet and the Bitter: Death and Dying in J. R. R. Tolkien's 'The Lord of the Rings'*. Kindle Edition, Kent State University Press, 2018.

Atkinson, David William. *The English Ars Moriendi*. Peter Lang, 1992.

Bailey, F. Amos. 'I Am Not Afraid of Dying. I Just Don't Want To Be There When It Happens'. *Medical Care*, vol. 46, no. 12, 2008, pp. 1195–97.

Breebaart, Leo, and Mike Kew, editors. *The Annotated Pratchett File v9.0*. The L-Space Web, 24 Aug. 2016, https://www.lspace.org/books/apf/.

Byatt, A. S. "Review: "Night Watch" - a Comforting Way of Death." *The Guardian*, 9 Nov. 2002. *The Guardian*, www.theguardian.com/books/2002/nov/09/sciencefictionfantasyandhorror.asbyatt.

Chraïbi, Aboubakr. *Contes Nouveaux Des 1001 Nuits: Étude Du Manuscrit Reinhardt*. Librairie d'Amérique et d'Orient: J. Maisonneuve, 1996.

Digg. "Every On-Screen Death In The "Lord Of The Rings" Trilogy, Extended Edition." *YouTube*, 10 Dec. 2014, https://www.youtube.com/watch?v=NfdKuSgXejI.

Gilbey, John. "Fantastic Voyager." *The Times Higher Education Supplement*, no. 1965, Sept. 2010, p. 34.

Marzolph, Ulrich, et al., editors. "The Story of King Sabâ." *The Arabian Nights Encyclopedia*, vol. 1, ABC-CLIO, 2004, pp. 354–56.

Maugham, W. Somerset. "Sheppey." *Collected Plays*, vol. 3, Heinemann, 1952, pp. 183–304.

---. *Sheppey, a Play in Three Acts*. William Heinemann, 1933.

Morrison, Jim. "An American Prayer." *The American Night: The Writings of*

Jim Morrison, Vol. 2, Vintage, 1991, pp. 1–18.

Morrison, Jim, and The Doors. *An American Prayer*. 1978. Elektra/Asylum Records, 1978.

Penny, Laurie. 'Sex, Death and Nature'. *New Statesman*, vol. 141, no. 5132, Nov. 2012, pp. 26–31.

Pratchett, Estate of Sir Terry, and Paul Kidby. *Terry Pratchett: His World*. 16 Sept. 2017–14 Jan. 2018, www.salisburymuseum.org.uk/whats-on/exhibitions/terry-pratchett-hisworld. Salisbury Museum.

Pratchett, Terry. 'A Genuine Absent-Minded Professor (Inaugural Professorial Lecture, Trinity College, Dublin, 4 November 2010)'. *A Slip of the Keyboard: Collected Non-Fiction*, Corgi Transworld, 2015, pp. 264–91.

---. *A Slip of the Keyboard: Collected Non-Fiction*. Corgi Transworld, 2015.

---. 'AT LAST, SIR TERRY, WE MUST WALK TOGETHER.' *@terryandrob*, 12 Mar. 2015, https://twitter.com/terryandrob/status/576036599047258112.

---. *Interesting Times*. Corgi, 1995.

---. "Kevins ("The Author", Winter 1993)." *A Slip of the Keyboard: Collected Non-Fiction*, Corgi Transworld, 2015, pp. 100–05.

---. 'Letter to J.R.R. Tolkien (22 November 1967)'. *Tolkien: Maker of Middle-Earth*, Bodleian Library, 2018, pp. 102–03.

---. *Mort*. Corgi, 1987.

---. *Night Watch*. Corgi, 2003.

---. *Reaper Man*. Corgi, 1992.

---. *Shaking Hands with Death*. Corgi Books, 2015.

---. *Small Gods*. Corgi, 1993.

---. *Soul Music*. Corgi, 1995.

---. 'Terry Took Death's Arm and Followed Him through the Doors and on to the Black Desert under the Endless Night.' *@terryandrob*, 12 Mar. 2015, https://twitter.com/terryandrob/status/576036726046646272.

---. *The Colour of Magic*. Corgi, 1984.

---. 'The End.' *@terryandrob*, 12 Mar. 2015, https://twitter.com/terryandrob/status/576036888190038016.

---. 'The Richard Dimbleby Lecture: Shaking Hands with Death (Royal Society of Medicine [Sic], Later Broadcast on BBC1, 1 February 2010)'. *A Slip of the Keyboard: Collected Non-Fiction*, Corgi Transworld, 2015, pp. 333–55.

---. *The Shepherd's Crown*. Doubleday, 2015.

Russell, Charlie. *Terry Pratchett: Back in Black*. BBC Two, 11 Feb. 2017.

'Sir Terry Pratchett: Shaking Hands with Death'. *The Richard Dimbleby Lecture*, 34, BBC 1, 1 Feb. 2010.

'Terry Pratchett: By the Book'. *The New York Times*, 17 Aug. 2014, p. 8.

Tolkien, J. R. R. "Athrabeth Finrod Ah Andreth." *Morgoth's Ring: The Later Silmarillion, Part One: The Legends of Aman*. Edited by Christopher Tolkien, HarperCollins, 1993, pp. 301–66.

---. "On Fairy-Stories." *Tree and Leaf*. Harper Collins Publishers, 2001, pp. 1–81.

---. *The Letters of J. R. R. Tolkien: A Selection*. Edited by Humphrey Carpenter, Houghton Mifflin, 2000.

---. *The Lord of the Rings*. 2nd reset edition, Harper Collins, 2002.

---. *The Silmarillion*. Houghton Mifflin, 1977.

Also Sprach Fëanor, Spirit of Fire: A Nietzschean Reading of Tolkien's Mythology?

Giovanni Carmine Costabile

No doubt is conceivable about Tolkien's own religion. He was raised by his mother Mabel as a devout Roman Catholic, and after she died, as Humphrey Carpenter writes, 'he associated her with his membership of the Catholic Church' (*Biography*, 50). To him, then, religion was no abstraction, but a real person. It could be speculated that the Grace of God was incarnate for him.

Nonetheless, his use of 'the Dark Lord' with the Lord capitalised in *The Lord of the Rings*, no matter how prevalent the adjective qualifying the noun, can be read as some sort of reference to the only God of the Judaeo-Christian tradition.

Naturally, this will sound strange, since Sauron, to whom the title refers, is the evil tyrant who rebelled against the figure who most closely approximates the Christian God, i.e. Eru Ilúvatar. Nonetheless, I decided to follow this hint which led me to question the canonical view of Tolkien's benevolent forces being an equivalent of the Heavenly Host. What if Eru was not God and instead Sauron and Melkor were his representatives? While this made no sense in a Christian, nor in a Jewish, perspective, there is a philosophy in which such an association might make sense. This was Friedrich Nietzsche's philosophy.

As Sauron is the master of the land of Mordor, where the shadows lie, so Nietzsche claims:

> After Buddha was dead people showed his shadow for centuries afterwards in a cave, – an immense frightful shadow. God is dead: – but as the human race is constituted, there will perhaps be caves for millenniums yet, in which people will show his shadow. – And we – we have still to overcome his shadow![1]

Friedrich Nietzsche was the proponent of a philosophical atheism and, by announcing God's death first in his 1882 *The Gay Science* and then, most relevantly, in his 1891 *Also Sprach Zarathustra* (*Thus Spoke Zarathustra*), he is often portrayed as the chief initiator of Postmodernism (Silverman and Delton, 212) and the "genuine critique of morality" (Leiter, 252). Alongside Sigmund Freud and Karl Marx, he is considered one out of the three "masters of suspicion" (Ricoeur, 32).

He could then well seem completely at odds with any attempt to associate him with Tolkien, but there are two more aspects to consider which are very important. First of all, even if we were to decide that Nietzsche had nothing in common with Tolkien, still as an influential figure in shaping, however possibly against his own intentions, the course of the 20th century intellectual and factual history, Nietzsche must surely have been in some way known to Tolkien, who could also have discussed him with C.S. Lewis, who was interested in Philosophy.

Secondly, some points in common between Nietzsche and

---

1. Friedrich Nietzsche. *The Gay Science*. Edited by Walter Kaufmann, Random House, 1974, p. 167.

Tolkien can be found through closer observation. On one hand, both were recognized philologists in their respective fields, Classics for Nietzsche, Germanic Philology for Tolkien.[2] On the other, both were strongly influenced by 19th century Romanticism[3] and held music, among the arts, in special consideration: Nietzsche composed music himself, highly praised it in his early 1872 work *The Birth of Tragedy* and was a close friend of the influential German composer Richard Wagner before their controversial and heated disagreement; Tolkien devised a creation myth based on music in his *Ainulindalë*, whose first version dates back to 1919-20, which has been supposed to constitute a negative commentary on Post-Romantic evolutions of symphonic music towards atonality, also influenced by the same Wagner[4], whose music Tolkien knew and discussed with C.S. Lewis and his brother in the early 1930s and whose ideology Tolkien strove to contrast in his mature works.[5]

As I previously mentioned, Nietzsche announced the death of God, thereby meaning that in his opinion science had made what he calls the hypothesis of God useless. On the contrary,

2. Discussed by Peter M. Candler Jr. in the chapter "Tolkien or Nietzsche: Philology and Nihilism" in Wood, Ralph C. (ed.), *Tolkien among the Moderns*. University of Notre Dame Press, 2015.

3. On Tolkien and Romanticism, see Julian Eilmann. *Tolkien Romanticist and Poet*. Walking Tree Publishers, 2017.

4. See Reuven Naveh. "The Ainulindalë and Tolkien's approach to Modernity" in *The Return of the Ring: Proceedings of the Tolkien Society Conference 2012*, Vol. 2, ed. by Lynn Forest Hill. Luna Press Publishing, 2016, pp. 101-110.

5. See Christine Chism. "Middle-earth, the Middle Ages and the Aryan Nation: Myth and History in the World War II" in *Tolkien the Medievalist*, ed. by Jane Chance. Routledge, 2003, pp. 63-89.

Nietzsche maintained that the Christian faith was a disease of the spirit, because he identified it with the ascetic ideal, whose contempt of the flesh Nietzsche could not tolerate. In fact, in Part 3, Aphorism 46 of *Beyond Good and Evil* he writes: 'From the beginning, Christian faith has been sacrifice: sacrifice of all freedom, of all pride, of all self-confidence of the spirit; it is simultaneously enslavement and self-derision, self-mutilation' (*Beyond Good and Evil*, 44).

Nonetheless, it was a fact that Christianity had been the driving force shaping the last nineteen centuries of European history, therefore he had somehow to explain how could a disease have become the norm, and such a successful one, too. Therefore, in *The Genealogy of Morality*, Nietzsche endeavours to reconstruct how from the ancient master morality, wherein the strong prevailed over the weak, we could get to what he terms the slave morality, or the idea that an Otherworldly compensation will repay the good and just who had no power in this life and punish the unfit rulers who mistreated and tormented them.

Nietzsche argued that the turning point between these two moralities had been the predication of St. Paul of Tharsus, who according to him was the true founder of Christianity rather than Jesus, interpreted as a simple rebel against the authority of the Temple of Jerusalem, guilty of recognizing Roman supremacy. But such a predication had only been possible as arising from the context of Judaism, whence Jesus came, therefore it was the Jews in general that had to be blamed.

It is worth to mention that, while in the *Genealogy* Nietzsche seems to have an openly anti-Semitic position, one such as Wagner also had, the argument is controversial, since Nietzsche openly rejected Wagner's anti-Semitism and in other works praised the Jews. Obviously one needs to be cautious when considering the fact that Nietzsche's philosophy, however unwillingly, contributed to shaping the Nazi ideology.

However, making the Jews responsible called Moses into question, since it was him who, according to Nietzsche, had invented the Ten Commandments, written on the Tables of Law. By making the biblical account a metaphor for the establishment of moral values, Nietzsche appropriated the symbol without recognizing its biblical meaning, and said we should break the Old Tables in order to write New Tables, although it may be difficult and in fact it has been difficult to critics to understand why should we abandon rules such as: "Thou shall not kill".

Nietzsche's comment in this respect, although probably hardly agreeable, in Book 1, Aphorism 26 of *The Gay Science*, states:

> What is life? Life - that is: continually shedding something that wants to die. Life - that is: being cruel and inexorable against everything about us that is growing old and weak -and not only about us. Life - that is, then: being without reverence for those who are dying, who are wretched, who are ancient? Constantly being a murderer? -And yet old Moses said: "Thou shalt not kill (*The Gay Science*, 100).

Nietzsche's major work, *Also Sprach Zarathustra* or *Thus Spoke Zarathustra* introduces a third character, the titular Zarathustra, or Zoroaster, the founder of Zoroastrism, as the original character responsible for, in Nietzsche's opinion, inventing the very idea of morality as based on the concepts of good and bad, or good and evil. Based on the same notion,

Nietzsche wrote that everything which is done out of love is beyond good and evil.

Nietzsche's Zarathustra returns after many centuries to correct his original mistake of morality, and therefore preaches amorality or even immorality as a key of elevation for Man, who might subsequently become the Superman as soon as he frees himself (Nietzsche has a male reader, or perhaps I should say disciple, in mind) from the alleged chains of moral judgement.

Therefore we have three figures whom Nietzsche considers responsible for morality: Zarathustra, initiator of morality; Moses, writer of the Law; and St. Paul, inventor of Christianity; to whom we could add a fourth figure, Nietzsche's personal Zarathustra as distinguished from the historical one, who fictitiously comes down from the top of his mountain in order to announce the end of morality and the new order of joy, liberty and godlessness.

While Tolkien, as I said, no doubt would not have agreed with any of these claims by Nietzsche, I would argue that he was aware of his philosophy and that a commentary thereupon is readable in his mythology. After all, Nietzsche was highly influential to the 20th century intellectual and factual history, therefore it would be absurd if Tolkien had not had some knowledge and opinion about his thought.

In fact, besides any Biblical and mythological reference possible, the character of Fëanor is readable as Tolkien's reworking of the philosophical motifs underlined by Nietzsche in his reading of Moses, St. Paul and the historical Zarathustra/ Zoroaster as well as his concept of the Superman. Fëanor in fact exhibits what can be seen as pure Superman-like traits when he is first described in *The Silmarillion*:

...Fëanor grew swiftly, as if a secret fire were kindled within him. He was tall, and fair of face, and masterful, his eyes piercingly bright and his hair raven-dark; in the pursuit of all his purposes eager and steadfast. Few ever changed his courses by counsel, none by force. He became of all the Noldor, then or after, the most subtle in mind and the most skilled in hand (*The Silmarillion*, 64).

How better to comment this description in the light of Fëanor's subsequent evolution, than by citing Nietzsche's remark: 'To demand of strength that it should not express itself as strength, that it should not be a desire to overcome, a desire to throw down, a desire to become master, a thirst for enemies and resistances and triumphs, is just as absurd as to demand of weakness that it should express itself as strength' (*The Genealogy of Morality*, 45).

The Noldorin lord surely later desired to overcome and to throw down Morgoth, as much as he desired to be the master of his people, the Noldor. 'A thirst for enemies and resistances and triumphs' is apparently also what drives him from Valinor to Middle-earth. By the way, such a statement as the one just cited could constitute a meaningful sort of commentary to Frodo's failure in *The Lord of the Rings* just as well, since all of the afore-cited desires are exactly those which the Ring causes, as it can be seen by examining Boromir's case.

Nonetheless, despite this apparent agreement, Tolkien thought that power was not the final answer, that there was something greater than power: the love made visible by the Grace of the Eldar and Valar; whereas Nietzsche deemed the Will to Power to be the ultimate key to reality. Therefore the diagnosis in both cases is the same: Man is power-sick. But the prognosis is different, because in Tolkien's case it could be identified in the evangelical 'love thy neighbour', while in Nietzsche's philosophy it would chiefly consist in the joyous acceptation of the sickness itself through *amor fati*, or even not seeing it as sickness at all.

Fëanor is readable as Tolkien's commentary on all the figures of Nietzsche's lawmakers: Zarathustra, Moses and St. Paul. Zarathustra is both the historical figure and Nietzsche's imaginary prophet who returns to correct its former mistake. About the former, very little is known apart from him being the founder of Zoroastrism, the first dualistic religion which opposed a divine figure of light and goodness, Ahura Mazda, to an equally divine but opposite deity of evil and darkness, Angra Manyu.

In a parallel way, Fëanor is the only character in Tolkien's Legendarium who establishes a precise norm of behaviour, which for our purposes is the equivalent of a Moral Law, when he convinces, or rather compels, all his sons to pronounce the Oath with him. As we read in *The Silmarillion*:

Then Fëanor swore a terrible oath. His seven sons leapt straightway to his side and took the selfsame vow together, and red as blood shone their drawn swords in the glare of the torches. They swore an oath which none shall break, and none should take, by the name even of Ilúvatar, calling the Everlasting Dark upon them if they kept it not; and Manwë they named in witness, and Varda, and the hallowed mountain of Taniquetil, vowing to pursue with vengeance and hatred to the Ends of the World Vala, Demon, Elf or Man as yet unborn, or any creature, great or small, good or evil, that time should bring forth unto the end of days, whoso should hold or take or keep a Silmaril from their possession (*Silmarillion*, 88 – 89).

From then on, Fëanor and his seven sons, and, in a lesser fashion, the rest of the Noldor, who witness the oath being pronounced, consider any given possibility of action in the light of their terrible oath. Many of the subsequent tragedies of Noldorin history, if not all of them, depend on the fact that the protagonists have to keep the oath. In a similar way, Nietzsche claims that once the concepts of moral good and moral evil were created, as distinguished from the good and bad of the masters, all of what was truly noble and good began to fail. This is an interesting parallel; however, I will treat Nietzsche's imaginary Zarathustra, as distinguished from the historical one, later.

In fact it is even more interesting to compare Fëanor to Moses: both are leaders of their respective peoples; both live in a period after their peoples moved to a foreign country and dwelt therein; both feel themselves and their peoples to be oppressed, mistreated and unjustly forced to stay in the foreign country (although Moses has much more reason to feel this way); both defy the foreign country's rulers and gods; both leave the foreign country; both are involved in a massacre by the sea of the foreigners who opposed their leave-taking; as also in Zarathustra's case, both are the Moral lawmakers of their peoples; finally both die in the immediate circumstance of reaching their respective promised lands.

There is a parallel involving God's role in their respective undertakings: as God, partly subconsciously, inspires Moses' actions, Fëanor's are inspired by Morgoth, partly through rumours spread among the Noldor, the source of which they do not themselves realise. An important difference, though, is that Fëanor is driven by hate for Morgoth, whereas Moses can only love and feel thankful to his Lord. But this does not negate all the other positive parallels.

In this reading, it is significant that the oath vows to 'pursue with vengeance and hatred' 'any creature, great or small, **good or evil**' (my emphasis). The oath does not take into account goodness or evil. The oath establishes a new criterion for judging good and evil, which consists in either giving the jewels to the Noldor, helping them to retrieve those (which is the new good), or hindering their retrieval, either actively or passively (which is the new evil). Therefore the oath is similar to what Nietzsche calls the subversion of the old values (i.e. good equals healthy and strong) and the establishment of new values (i.e. good equals miserable and humble), first operated by the Jews, then by the Christians.

The question is now obvious: why would a devout Catholic develop atheistic, anti-Christian motifs in his works, or at least allow some of us to read these motifs in them? I believe we have to turn to C.S. Lewis for an answer, which can hardly be better formulated:

> A man who disbelieved the Christian story as fact but continually fed on it as myth would, perhaps, be more spiritually alive than one who assented and did not think much about it. The modernist - the extreme modernist, infidel in all but name - need not be called a fool or hypocrite because he obstinately retains, even in the midst of his intellectual atheism, the language, rites, sacraments, and story of the Christians. The poor man may be clinging (with a wisdom he himself by no means understands) to that which is his life. It would have been better that Loisy should have remained a Christian: it would not necessarily have been better that he should have purged his thought of vestigial Christianity (Lewis, 67).

It is a good thing in a secular sense that a work may be

read by both Christians and atheists, and that it is an enriching experience for both. In a Christian view, according to C.S. Lewis, it is even better, and we might reasonably think that Tolkien agreed.

To conclude, in his aphorism 125 of *The Gay Science* Nietzsche suggests that, as a consequence of his theory of God's death, we should become gods ourselves:

> God is dead. God remains dead. And we have killed him. How shall we comfort ourselves, the murderers of all murderers? What was holiest and mightiest of all that the world has yet owned has bled to death under our knives: who will wipe this blood off us? What water is there for us to clean ourselves? What festivals of atonement, what sacred games shall we have to invent? Is not the greatness of this deed too great for us? Must we ourselves not become gods simply to appear worthy of it? (*The Gay Science*, 181)

But eventually I found that Tolkien himself explains why Morgoth and Sauron are each called the Dark Lord, with 'Lord' being capitalized as in God's case:

> In *The Lord of the Rings* the conflict is not basically about 'freedom', though that is naturally involved. It is about God, and His sole right to divine honour. The Eldar and the Númenóreans believed in the One, the true God, and held worship of any other person in abomination. Sauron desired to be a God-King, and was held to be this by his servants; if he had been victorious he would have demanded divine honour from all rational creatures and absolute temporal power over the whole world (*Letters*, Letter 183).

I suppose that Tolkien's personal view is clearly revealed by this statement, and there can be no doubt as to what Tolkien would say if asked why Sauron is comparable to a variant of the Lord: in fact, he can only be so in his own claim and arrogance.

The following passage in *Exodus* can be linked to the many instances of characters being rescued by Eagles in Tolkien's works, and therefore Eucatastrophe:

And Moses went up unto God, and the LORD called unto him out of the mountain, saying, Thus shalt thou say to the house of Jacob, and tell the children of Israel;
Ye have seen what I did unto the Egyptians, **and how I bare you on eagles' wings**, and brought you unto myself (*Exodus* 19, my emphasis).

Nietzsche is apparently unaware that the shadow of God is cited in the Bible, as well, and has an entirely different significance, symbolizing God's protection:

How precious is Your loving kindness, O God! And the children of men take refuge **in the shadow of Your wings** (*Psalms* 36, 7, my emphasis).

In fact in the desert a shadow under which to take refuge is indeed a good thing, as Isaiah testifies:

"For You have been a defense for the helpless,
A defense for the needy in his distress,
A refuge from the storm, **a shade from the heat**;
For the breath of the ruthless
Is like a rain storm against a wall"
(*Isaiah* 25, 4, my emphasis)

Instead no shadow which is intended as inconsistency is referred to God in the Bible because:

> Every good thing given and every perfect gift is from above, coming down from the Father of lights, with whom there is **no variation or shifting shadow** (*James* 1, 17, my emphasis).

Similarly in Tolkien, although the Grey Elves may be romanticized, the stress is on the light of Aman, coming from Eru; while Mordor is the land of shadows precisely because it is the farthest place from that light.

Of course, to claim Tolkien's Christianity and Catholicism as the most founded reading we have at the moment, and given the present evidence, should not constitute a reason to forbid any different reading in the applicability of a literary work, even an atheistic, Nietzschean, anti-Christian one. In the same way, the possibility of any other reading, which nobody wants to question, I hope, should not question the scientific fact that the Christian reading is the most well-founded in Tolkien's biography and correspondence, again, given the present evidence of the case.

That would be, in my opinion, the case, assuming that we have to choose and cannot apply Claudio Testi's "Christian and Pagan" synthetical approach, because for any reason the Christian and Pagan views collide, as it happened to Gawain in *Sir Gawain and the Green Knight*, according to Tolkien's own W. P. Ker lecture of 1953.

In that lecture the Professor had claimed that Sir Gawain in his Green Knight adventure had to choose between his allegiance to the chivalric code (which arguably can be considered as an equivalent of Paganism) and Christian morality, and, having chosen the latter, which according to Tolkien is superior and highest, he is innocent and devoid of any serious fault, even though, by keeping a green sash received as a gift from a lady, he had violated the rules of a Christmas game he had been playing with his courteous host.

However, it is far more common that knights can be both chivalric and Christian, and being chivalric they defend Christianity, and being Christian they are chivalrous; therefore also an interpretation of Tolkien's works can be both Pagan and Christian, without having to choose one way only in spite of the other.

Bibliography

Holy Bible King James Version. Collins, 1991.

Postmodernism and Continental Philosophy. Edited by Hugh J. Silverman and Donn Welton, SUNY Press, 1988.

Candler, Peter M. Jr. "Tolkien or Nietzsche: Philology and Nihilism." *Tolkien among the Moderns*. Edited by Ralph C. Wood, University of Notre Dame Press, 2015.

Carpenter, Humphrey. *J.R.R. Tolkien: A Biography*. Harper Collins, 2002.

Chism, Christine. "Middle-earth, the Middle Ages and the Aryan Nation: Myth and History in the World War II." *Tolkien the Medievalist*. Edited by Jane Chance, Routledge, 2003.

Eilmann, Julian. *Tolkien Romanticist and Poet*. Walking Tree Publishers, 2017.

Leiter, Brian. "Nietzsche and the Morality Critics." *Ethics*, vol. 107, no. 2, 1997, pp. 250-285.

Lewis, Clive Staples. *Myth Became Fact in God in the Dock*. Eerdmans, 1970.

Naveh, Reuven. "The Ainulindalë and Tolkien's approach to Modernity." *The Return of the Ring: Proceedings of the Tolkien Society Conference 2012*, vol. 2, edited by Lynn Forest-Hill. Luna Press Publishing, 2016, pp. 101-110.

Nietzsche, Friedrich. *Beyond Good and Evil*. Edited by Rolf-Peter Horstmann and Judith Norman, Cambridge University Press, 2002.

---. *Also sprach Zarathustra: Ein Buch für Alle und Keinen*. Ernst Schmeitzner, 1883–1891.

---. *The Gay Science*. Edited by Walter Kaufmann, Random House, 1974.

---. *The Genealogy of Morality*. Edited by Walter Kaufmann, Random House, 1989.

Ricoeur, Paul. *Freud and Philosophy*. An Essay on Interpretation. Yale University Press, 2008.

Tolkien, J. R. R. *The Letters of J.R.R. Tolkien*. Edited by Humphrey Carpenter with the assistance of Christopher Tolkien, Houghton Mifflin, 2000.

---. *The Silmarillion*. Houghton Mifflin, 1977.

About the Contributors

Ryan Haecker is a PhD student in the Faculty of Divinity at the University of Cambridge. He has been awarded the Peterhouse Graduate Research Studentship to study philosophical theology under the supervision of Professor Lord Rowan Williams of Oystermouth. His doctoral dissertation, tentatively titled 'Restoring Reason: Origen's Trinitarian Logic', should show, through a deep and creative reading of Origen of Alexandria, how logic is ontological, ontology is theological, and theology is trinitarian. He has previously studied history, philosophy, and theology at the University of Texas, the University Würzburg, and the University of Nottingham. His research explores the intersections of ancient Platonism, medieval Scholasticism, and modern Idealism for modern theology.

Markus Altena Davidsen recently wrote a PhD dissertation entitled "The Spiritual Tolkien Milieu: A Study of Fiction-based Religion" (defended 2014), about an international network of spiritual groups that take all or most of their inspiration from Tolkien's works. In addition to the dissertation, he published a number of articles on Tolkien-based spirituality and is currently preparing a monograph version of his dissertation, which will appear in 2019 on De Gruyter under the title Tolkien Spirituality: Constructing Belief and Tradition in Fiction-based Religion.

Aslı Bülbül Candaş is a PhD student in English Literature at Cardiff Metropolitan University. She received her BA in English Language and Literature from İstanbul University and MA in English Literature from İstanbul Aydın University. In her MA she explored the concepts of multiculturalism, individuality and cultural history in *The Lord of the Rings*. Her PhD is on studying the concept of perfection in Tolkien's secondary world through the concepts of art, space, time and fate. She has been a member of The Tolkien Society since 2015.

Justin Lewis-Anthony is deputy director of the Anglican Centre in Rome, the Archbishop of Canterbury's representation to the Holy See. He was formally a research fellow at Ripon College, Cuddesdon, Oxford, and for three years Dean of Students at Virginia Theological Seminary in the United States. He is the author of three books on popular and high culture and theology (Circles of Thorns, If You Meet George Herbert on the Road, and You Are the Messiah, And I Should Know), all published by Bloomsbury/Continuum, and is editor of a new monograph series for T&T Clark on Contemporary Writers and Their Theology. He is completing another book for Bloomsbury on silence (Lazarus In The Arctic).

Giovanni Carmine Costabile holds an Mphil in Philosophy from the Università della Calabria in Italy. Independent scholar, freelance translator and private teacher, he has published on Tolkien and Medieval Literature on the journal of Tolkien Studies (XIV, 2017), on Inklings Jahrbuch (34, 2017) and in the Peter Roe series of the Tolkien Society (Death and Immortality, 2017), besides for Limina Mentis in Italy (2016/2018). He presented papers at the Tolkien Seminar 2016 in Leeds, at Raduno Tolkieniano 2017 in San Marino, at Oxonmoot 2017 and at the NUME roundtable in October of the same year in Florence. As a translator he published an authorized Italian version of an essay by Verlyn Flieger on Tolkien scholar and research-partner Oronzo Cilli's webpage Tolkieniano (April 2017). He takes delight in writing short stories and composing poetry and songs, and he published a selection of his poems in a book titled "Lingue di te" (Aletti, 2017), besides being nominated "Federician Poet" for being a finalist at the poetry contest "Il Federiciano" in Italy.

Lightning Source UK Ltd.
Milton Keynes UK
UKHW012323030319
338405UK00002B/36/P

9 781911 143796